The Trials of ERIC MAREO

The Trials of
ERIC MAREO

Charles Ferrall
& Rebecca Ellis

Victoria University Press

VICTORIA UNIVERSITY PRESS
Victoria University of Wellington
PO Box 600 Wellington

© Charles Ferrall & Rebecca Ellis 2002

ISBN 0 86473 432 8

First published 2002

National Library of New Zealand Cataloguing-in-Publication Data
Ferrall, Charles.
The trials of Eric Mareo / Charles Ferrall & Rebecca Ellis.
Includes bibliographical references and index.
ISBN 0-86473-432-8
1. Mareo, Eric, 1892-1960—Trials, litigation, etc. 2. Trials
(Murder)—New Zealand—History—20th century. 3. Judicial error—
New Zealand—History—20th century. I. Ellis, Rebecca. II. Title.
345.9302523—dc 21

Printed by PrintLink, Wellington

Contents

For Thomasina and Nell

And in memory of Kim Walker

Preface

IF, AS PAUL VALÉRY MAINTAINED, a poem is never finished only abandoned, perhaps books are never begun only resumed. We decided to write this book several years ago when, returning to Wellington from a holiday, Rebecca remembered that her father had once suggested that she consider writing an LLM thesis on the Mareo case. Although her father was too young to remember the trials, they were nevertheless a familiar part of the legal landscape in which he practised law. There was also a personal connection through the Ellis family's friendship with H.G.R. Mason, a major protagonist in this story, who was himself writing a book about the trials when he died in 1975.

After an initial foray into the files, it became apparent that R v Mareo was a poor subject for post-graduate legal study. It contained too little in the way of interest to academic lawyers, and far too much in the way of interest of a more diverting kind. The LLM was shelved.

In the five years that followed our rekindled enthusiasm for the subject, the name Freda Stark became more widely known in New Zealand. Although her involvement in Mareo's trials was very much a part of Stark's story, it seemed to us that what had been told about them in that context raised as many questions as it answered. In that way, history's recent love affair with Freda only fortified our pre-existing resolve to attempt to present the whole Eric Mareo story.

So we are grateful to Justice Tony Ellis for the initial inspiration, and to those others who helped us resume and complete the task. Sir Trevor Henry gave generously of his time and phenomenal recall on two occasions. James Hollings, Jane Stafford and Anne McCarthy read early drafts and made helpful suggestions for revisions. In particular we would like to thank Judith Dale for her scrupulous attention to weaknesses in an earlier version. Brent Parker provided invaluable archival assistance, and Philip Braithwaite followed some leads for us in London, as did Charles's father, John Ferrall, in Sydney. Thanks also to Mary Moll and Allan Brownlee, Thelma Mareo's relatives, for generously sharing some family history and photos, and to Jan Crane and Michael Quinn in Australia for their information on the Pechotsch family. Redmer Yska was a continual source of enthusiasm and guidance. Ashley Heenan, Peter Walls, and Allan Thomas gave us valuable advice on musical matters. Belinda Ellis somehow managed to design the cover despite the input of two opinionated relatives. Thanks also to Roger Robinson for finding us some research money, Bill Manhire for guiding us to Fergus Barrowman and to the latter and Sue Brown for their splendid editing work.

As an academic and a lawyer we thought we were able to correct each other's weaknesses – but in ways we can't specify without slandering both our professions. Nevertheless, we must thank the domestic god or gods who allowed our own family to survive the process of writing a book about the disintegration of another.

Introduction

WHEN THE JURY'S VERDICT of 'Guilty' was flashed on the cinema screen on 17 June 1936, the Auckland audience rose from their seats and cheered. The person whose fate had just been decided was the flamboyant 45-year-old musician Eric Mareo and the crime for which he had been convicted was the murder of his second wife of only eighteen months, Thelma, a 29-year-old Australian actress and singer. According to the Crown, Mareo had laced a glass of milk with a sleeping draught, a barbiturate called veronal, and given it to his wife. His alleged motive: to replace Thelma with his young musical assistant, Eleanor Brownlee.

But this was not the only love triangle to emerge from the trial. Soon after her arrival in New Zealand, Thelma had met a young Auckland woman called Freda Stark, a chorus girl employed in the musical in which she was starring in Hamilton. They soon became close friends, Stark later spending weekends at the Mareos' house in the respectable Auckland suburb of Mt Eden. Although Stark had not stayed the night at the Mareos' on the fatal long weekend of 12–15 April 1935, she had been present when Mareo allegedly poisoned his wife, even helping Thelma to drink the glass of milk in which Mareo had supposedly dissolved the lethal draught of veronal. On their own these facts would have ensured that Stark's testimony at the trial would be crucial. However, it had also been revealed earlier that soon after Thelma's death Mareo had told the police that his wife was 'fonder of women than of men, if you know what I mean' and that she and Stark had been 'lesbian' lovers.[1] Not surprisingly, then, Stark was the key witness at the trial, Mareo even dramatically claiming, when asked by the first trial judge if he had any final words after the jury's verdict had been delivered, that he had 'been sentenced on the lying word of Freda Stark'.[2]

Mareo was then sentenced to death. As he was being led from the courtroom he looked towards his convent-educated daughter, 21-year-old Betty, and said her name twice. Betty had also given testimony at the trial, although she had not been staying at the house over the fateful weekend. However, she had a younger, 17-year-old brother, Graham, who was present when Thelma drank the glass of milk and who not only contradicted Stark's evidence in court on crucial issues but testified that his stepmother had been a heavy drinker and frequently bedridden for days on end.

Obviously, this was no ordinary trial. Between the wars there were on average only two murders a year in New Zealand and the Mareos' 'Bohemian type of existence', according to one eyewitness, although 'no more facinorous [sic], or even unusual, than what might have been derived from the lives of hundreds, perhaps thousands, of theatrical people in the older cities of the world' was largely unfamiliar to an 'insular, colonial people, living for the most part in God's fresh air'.[3] Moreover, this had not been Mareo's only trial. Public interest had already been fuelled by the preliminary hearing in the Police Court between 29 September and 3 October 1935, and then in the first trial in the Auckland Supreme Court from 17 to 26 February 1936. While Mareo was in the Condemned Cell for the first time evidence had come to hand of sufficient weight and relevance to justify a successful application for retrial. Thus public interest in the lives of the Mareos had been gaining momentum for some time when, during the closing stages of the second trial, according to the same eyewitness,

a crowd of several hundred people surged round the Court outside, eager to find a way in. The conduct of some of the women who formed themselves into a four-deep queue at a side door was remarkable. They fought, they scrambled, they pushed, they elbowed each other in their efforts to retain their place in the queue. One who showed a little more temper and determination than any of the others was forcibly removed by a policeman.[4]

But Mareo did not hang, in part because the second trial judge, Mr Justice Callan, had written confidentially to the Attorney-General and Minister of Justice, H.G.R. Mason, expressing his concern that by the end of the trial he 'could not finally convince [himself] of Mareo's guilt'.[5] Mareo, then, remained in gaol while a small, diverse and at times eccentric band of supporters proclaimed his innocence and campaigned for his release in the newspapers, Select Committee hearings, Cabinet, Parliament, and eventually an appellate courtroom. Mareo's case was even taken up later by Mason, much to the annoyance of most of his officials and colleagues, including the Prime Minister Peter Fraser, whom Mason was later to describe as a sadist in his treatment of those who opposed him within the party.[6] Notwithstanding the varied and strenuous efforts on his behalf, he served the usual 'life' sentence, eventually being released on probation – only to meet with more controversy involving yet another woman. And, while perhaps in the normal course of events his name would have gradually faded from memory following his death, he is still remembered by many because of his role in the life of his nemesis, Freda Stark. As is well known, after the trials Stark became even better known as the 'Fever of the Fleet', a role which required her to dance before American GIs during the Second World War clad only in a G-string and gold paint, eventually becoming, before her death in 1999, not just a gay and lesbian 'icon' but, according to one of her friends, 'almost postage stamp stuff'[7] to the rest of New Zealand. Given changing attitudes towards homosexuality since the 1970s, it is not surprising, then, that most people today accept Stark's account of the trials.

But why did people believe her at the time of the trials? After all, there can be no doubt that New Zealand during the middle decades of the twentieth century was, like most other societies, homophobic. How could the public have believed in Mareo's guilt when such a belief rested largely upon the evidence of someone who qualified by the standards of the day as a 'sexual pervert', and whose testimony was far from uncontradicted? Moreover, the Crown's medical evidence was weak. For example, the case against Mareo rested on a medical principle supposedly propounded by the world's foremost toxicologist, Sir William Willcox, and yet when Sir William himself concluded in 1941 that Mareo could not have poisoned his wife both his expertise and competence were called into question.

Although we do want to clear the name of Mareo, that is not the main purpose of this book. In part this book is a 'who done it', but it is also an attempt to solve a far greater mystery: why the vast majority of New Zealanders believed in Mareo's guilt. The trials were a kind of drama, particularly because its two main actors were such consummate performers. However, the play that unfolded before the public eye in the courtrooms was just a part of a much larger social drama.[8] Just as Claudius's reaction to Hamlet's play 'The Mousetrap' demonstrates his bad conscience, so the reaction of most New Zealanders to the drama that unfolded in the courtrooms was also revealing. In attempting to explain why the jury reached its verdict to the applause of most of the New Zealand public, we are also hoping to describe important aspects of New Zealand society during the Depression, and perhaps beyond. As well as being a 'who done it', this book is also social history. As Hamlet might have said, the trials of Eric Mareo did indeed 'hold, as 'twere, the mirror up to nature'.

CHAPTER ONE

'A Very Experienced Man of the World': The Crown's Case

ALTHOUGH NEW ZEALAND had been on the international entertainment circuit since the 1860s, according to a local musician in 1934 'in this remote corner of the earth' celebrated musicians invariably caused 'a great stir in the community'.[1] This seems to have been particularly so in the years just before Eric Mareo's arrival in Wellington, at least judging by the popularity of visiting companies. According to one historian, the 1920s was a 'golden age' for touring companies with 'a greater variety of stage shows in New Zealand during the years 1920 to 1930, than ever before or since'.[2]

Moreover, even classically-trained musicians such as Mareo would have performed popular works to not always exclusive audiences. Although some cultural historians have argued that this period, the so-called 'Modernist' era, was characterised by what is often called a 'great divide' between 'mass' and 'high' culture, the musical world from which the Mareos had come was far less divided.[3] As well as having conducted classical music, Mareo had, for example, performed in British music halls. Besides, this 'great divide' was far less pronounced in a country of only about one and a half million people. The country could not support either a professional theatre or orchestra and, according to Adrienne Simpson, the widening of the gap between 'high' and 'comic' opera 'occurred more slowly in New Zealand' than most other Western countries.[4] A musician like Mareo could therefore expect to enjoy both the cultural prestige of the classical musician and the popularity of the entertainer.

And Mareo was a particularly versatile and energetic musician. As the musical director of the famous Australian musical company the Ernest C. Rolls Revue, he had arrived in

Auckland in September 1933 with Thelma Trott and 200 tons of theatrical equipment. The company performed two extravagant revues – one, according to a reviewer, 'filled with snappy dancing, some really spectacular scenes, and some comedy hits of hilarious quality'.[5] After touring the North Island with this company he married Thelma, left the company, returned to Auckland, secured the services of 45 musicians, and rehearsed and conducted the first performance of the Mareo Symphony Orchestra. In the course of several concerts, the orchestra performed such standards from our classical repertoire as Beethoven's Fifth and Ninth symphonies, the latter with a choir of 150 voices, Ravel's *Bolero* (which had never been performed in the southern hemishere, and which Mareo needed to transcribe from a gramophone recording), and Lalo's *Symphonie Espagnole* with the noted New Zealand violinist Vincent Aspey as soloist. However, more surprising was the orchestra's performance of Gershwin's *Rhapsody in Blue*, a piece which was 'acclaimed by critics and public alike to the dismay of those musicians who had contended that Mareo was lowering the prestige of his orchestra in performing it'.[6] Less than a year later Mareo had formed the Mareo Operatic Society and staged Ivan Caryll's *The Duchess of Danzig*, a light opera set in the Napoleonic period and featuring Thelma Mareo in one of the principal parts as a washerwoman who befriends the 'Little Corporal' 'when his fortunes were at their lowest ebb, and who later, as the wife of one of his great generals, becomes the Duchess of Danzig'.[7] Just after the last performance of *The Duchess*, Mareo was employed by the St James Theatre to conduct a pared-down orchestra during the screening of films. At the time of his arrest, he was collaborating with a judge of the Native Land Court, Frank Acheson, to adapt his novel *Plume of the Arawas*, a historical romance set in pre-colonial New Zealand, into a £20,000 movie. Mareo claimed to have 'written over seven hundred works, many of which are recorded for the gramophone'.[8] These works were both 'serious' and 'light' and were published under seven different names because, as he told a reporter, 'in England, they won't allow you to be versatile. They think a man who can write a symphony ought not to be able to write light stuff'.[9] Like some kind of modern-day Proteus, Mareo was not only keen to assume any kind of musical role but he was in a country that apparently provided him with that opportunity.

It seems his audiences were not disappointed. The *New Zealand Radio Record* reported that the first performance of the Mareo Symphony Orchestra 'was an outstanding success musically, and was a triumph for Mr Eric Mareo . . . who proved that his great courage and determination to form such an organisation was well founded'.[10] It then went on to observe that the second half of the concert was broadcast live by a local radio station to an audience who 'were agreeably surprised at the high standard of the orchestra's work'.[11] The Mayor of Auckland had promised to introduce Mareo and his orchestra at this concert but had been detained in Wellington. Nevertheless, he 'sent a telegram, which was read, expressing regret for his absence and commending the orchestra and wishing it every success'.[12] About nine months later the premiere of *The Duchess of Danzig* was equally well received, the *New Zealand Herald* commending 'the sureness of principals, chorus and ballet', the 'lavish and spectacular scale' of the 'general staging', the 'strength' but not obtrusiveness of the orchestra and concluding with the observation that 'Mr Eric Mareo . . . was responsible not only for the musical direction, but for the general production of a most successful performance'.[13]

Even offstage, Mareo made a strong impression. Just prior to the first performance of his orchestra, a reporter from the *Observer* found that 'Mr Mareo is a genial soul . . . [who] amused me for an hour recounting some of his varied musical experiences'. These included a couple of no doubt well polished stories about a thirsty cornetist who was always 'harf a pint flat', a polite request distorted by members of an orchestra to an indignant bassoonist to 'hold yer —— row!!' and a cheap champagne dinner for fourteen in inflation-ravaged Leipzig just after the War.[14] Not only was Mareo adept at self-promotion but he was able to flatter the locals. He told the *Radio Record*, for example, that '[w]hen I came here first I immediately liked the city, particularly your fine harbour, as I am a keen yachting enthusiast'.[15]

More importantly, Mareo was able to inspire confidence in the local musicians. Even after the trials the *Observer* reported that a 'man who worked with him described him as "a sublime optimist"'[16] (a frequent observation) and that a 'prominent musician' is reported to have said that

> [h]e was a genius from start to finish. He could get you to do anything. He had a capacity for making any player, even if only a moderate performer, think he was really good, and we played for him like people possessed. He showed us new interpretations of old works, and there was an undeniable thrill in playing for him.[17]

The Mareos' Life Before the Fatal Weekend

Nevertheless, there was clearly another side to Mareo's professional life. *The Duchess of Danzig* had not been a financial success and its director was receiving no income at the time of his wife's death. Mareo's last job (according to the theatre's manager) had been 'to bring back some of the glamour of the days when depression was unheard of' by conducting an overture during 'the several tedious minutes' in which audiences would otherwise suffer through the 'credit titles'[18] at the St James Theatre. Since this was now the period of the talkies it is unlikely that audiences would have greatly appreciated the anachronistic supplement of live music. Moreover, as Ngaio Marsh famously observed, with the onset of the Depression, '[a]ll over Australasia one seemed to hear the desolate slam of stage doors'.[19] Thus Mareo's job at the St James lasted only six months. Two weeks after losing this job, Thelma was dead.

As the Crown made clear at the first trial, the apparent glamour of Mareo's life in fact rested on an unhappy marriage. Indeed according to the Crown's main witness, Freda Stark, the Mareos' marriage was all but over:

After the play [*The Duchess of Danzig*] finished we had a party out at Dixieland [on 13 October 1934] . . . It wasn't a very pleasant evening. We left before it was finished. – I mean Thelma and I left. We went home – to No. 1 Tenterden Av. When we got there we went to bed. In Thelma's room. I was staying there for the weekend. I remember the accused coming home – about an hour after us. Mrs Mareo and I were in bed when he came home. He was very drunk. He burst the door open. He came in and swore at Thelma. He said 'You bitch, you have insulted me in public. Here was I looking for my bloody wife and making a b—— fool of myself'. He told me to get out of bed, and go into Betty's room. I went to get out of bed but Thelma clung onto me. I did go into Betty's room. I was there only a few minutes when I heard a row in the front room. I heard a bang and Thelma came running down the passage to my room with Mr Mareo following her. She was crying, and holding her face. She said to me 'Don't let him get me.' I think Graham came into the room too while she was there and Mr Mareo, but I couldn't be sure. Mareo tried to bring his wife back to her room but she clung onto the bedclothes and wouldn't let go.

Mr Mareo went back into the front room himself and we followed. He said 'Look at you, you dirty drunken bitch. I used to drink tea till I met you. You b—— prostitute, get out into the streets where you belong.' Thelma said she would if he would give her back her [savings of] £500 [that Mareo had spent]. He said 'I can't, it will take me two years to pay it back.' He said 'You bought me with your £500.'

Mareo's condition at that time was that he was very hysterical. Graham was there in addition to Mrs Mareo and myself. Graham had to hit him in the chest – like to knock him down on the bed to quieten him. After he had quietened down Graham took him into the next bedroom. I stayed in with Thelma. For about – not more than half an hour. Then Mr Mareo came in and said he was quite all right and wanted to go to sleep. After that I went back to Betty's room and spent the night there. The Mareos were in their own room.[20]

A few months later, on the Saturday night of 17 February, the Mareos had another argument. Again Thelma and Stark were in bed together when Mareo came home drunk. On this second occasion, however, Eleanor Brownlee, who had been assisting Mareo with several of his musical and theatrical projects, accompanied him. Mareo came into their bedroom and, according to Stark, said

> 'I'm shot.' 'Eleanor has brought me home.' He meant he was drunk. Mrs Mareo said 'She can't stay the night. You knew Freda was staying here.' Mareo replied 'Oh, she can sleep anywhere.' He then left the room and went to the bathroom. Mrs Mareo and I went out to see Eleanor. We got up and went out to see what Eleanor was doing. She was in the sitting room, in her pyjamas, making up a bed between two chesterfield chairs. There was conversation. While that was going on we heard a bump – out by the bathroom. Thelma went down to the bathroom and we followed. I did not see the accused. I knew he was in the bathroom. Thelma went into the bathroom. She did not stay in there. Mr Mareo told her to get out. He said 'Eleanor can look after me.' Miss Brownlee pushed her way into the bathroom then. Thelma said 'You can't come in.' She said Mr Mareo was undressed. She did go into the bathroom. Mrs Mareo said then 'Oh, well, if that is the case I will leave' and she walked out of the bathroom. She said 'Oh come on, Freda, we won't stay the night here,' so I took her to my place in Prince Street. As she was going out of the door she said 'This is sufficient grounds for a divorce.' She said 'Oh, did you hear her call him Eric?'[21]

The next morning Thelma and Freda returned to the house with a suitcase and the intention of packing the former's possessions, but instead stayed the night. The following day Mareo gave Thelma a letter from Eleanor Brownlee apologising for the events of the previous evening. After reading the letter, Stark testified that Thelma said, 'That doesn't alter the fact. She won't be allowed to come to the house again.'[22] Even before this incident, Thelma had chastised her husband for his relations with Brownlee when he had been employed at the St James Theatre. According to Stark, Thelma had objected to 'Eleanor doing Mr Mareo's washing and cleaning out his dressing room at the Theatre . . . [o]n a number of occasions'.[23] Thus, according to A.H. Johnstone for the Crown, Mareo planned to replace his wife with Eleanor Brownlee:

A very experienced man of the world found a young girl who could be an extremely useful assistant, whose mission in life – at that time, at any rate – seemed to have been to perform every possible kind of service for him, menial or otherwise. He seemed almost to have cast some spell upon her. Her qualifications were similar to those of his own wife. They were both university graduates and they were musicians. Was it not that his own wife was now an encumbrance? And so, at the end of March, we find him [having lost his job at the St James] out of employment, married, an addict to drink, taking veronal every day, £500 of his wife's money spent . . . His wife was nothing to him sexually or financially.[24]

One month after the bathroom incident on 20 March a Dr Walton called on Thelma at home because '[s]he was in a highly nervous irritable worried condition' and prescribed her a sedative.[25] Four days later Mareo surprised Thelma and Stark in bed for a third time, when, according to the latter,

[a]ll of a sudden he burst in the door and said 'what are you doing?' He seemed in a very excited state and he had been drinking. When he calmed down he said 'Oh, Thelma I want to tell you something.' He said 'Freda, hurry up and go home.' I went home.[26]

Two days later on the Friday afternoon of 22 March Thelma visited Dr Walton at his consulting rooms. Dr Walton testified that Thelma's 'nervous condition' had deteriorated even further and that in particular '[s]he seemed to be unhappy in her married life. She said that her husband had made to her some unjust charges – untrue charges of some kind of perversion. She denied it'.[27] These charges had presumably been made on the third occasion when Mareo had surprised the two women in bed together. In one of his statements to the police, Mareo confessed that 'I did call my wife a Lesbyan [*sic*] on one occasion when I found my wife in bed with Freda Stark' but he did not specify on which of the three occasions he had made this accusation.[28] Soon after this consultation with Dr Walton, Thelma went to visit Mareo at the St James. Stark was also at the theatre and according to her she found Thelma

> in a very nervous state and . . . lying on a couch. She was very very pale and was trembling. Mr Mareo said to me 'Oh, all she needs is a feed'. As she got up to powder her face he wanted to give her a drink of brandy or whisky and she refused it.[29]

Six days later on 28 March Mareo lost his job at the St James. At about this time his daughter, Betty, left home after having quarrelled with Thelma, and Mareo purchased twenty-five veronal tablets. On 6 April he bought twelve more tablets of veronal followed by a further twenty tablets five days later from another chemist.

At the start of the trial the Crown called a number of witnesses to prove that Thelma had been in good health before the long weekend of her death. Stanley Porter, an insurance agent, testified that when he visited her on the previous Monday Thelma was doing some washing at the end of the verandah in the washhouse and 'seemed in her usual spirits'. Thelma asked Porter 'if I would be going anywhere near the Post Office and if so would I post a letter for her'.[30] On the same day a grocer's assistant by the name of Kenneth Bark called at the house in the morning, took a written order from Thelma, and delivered it later that afternoon. Bark delivered another order three days later and on both occasions found Thelma 'in her usual spirits'. Boris Thornton, a butcher's assistant, also saw Thelma 'once or twice' that week and told the court that '[s]he seemed to be in good health, just as usual'. Finally, Hubert Smith, a violinist in Mareo's orchestra, thought that Thelma 'seemed to be in good health' because she was able to climb onto a verandah rail and pick beans.[31]

The Fatal Long Weekend: Friday

On Friday 12 April Betty, who had left home about two weeks earlier, returned to Tenterden Avenue and was told by her father that Thelma was not well. Betty and Thelma passed each other once in the corridor but did not speak. At about six o'clock that evening, Betty, Mareo and Graham had a tea of reheated fish and chips. Betty then visited the neighbours. Upon returning she noticed that Thelma had cleaned all the dishes and gone back to bed. Just before she left, Mareo gave Betty a sealed letter with the instructions 'Only to Be Opened in the Event of My Death'. Betty said that '[a]t the time he was writing that letter and when he gave it to me I noticed that he was very worried'.[32] In the letter Mareo informed her that she was the 'legal' daughter of another man in England called Mr Gray. He concluded the letter

> . . . if anything happens to me communicate with Carn, solicitor, 13 Thames Street, Kingstone-on-Thames, England. I solemnly swear that what I am telling you now is the *absolute truth.* Altho' I have made a failure of my life I have tried to do the best I could for you, so think kindly of me if you can, sweetheart. I love you: God bless and protect you always – Your loving Daddy.

> P.S. – My advice is to take this letter to a solicitor and get his advice as to how to proceed, as it *must* be possible thru' a birthmark or records in the doctor's book or the nursing home to prove what I have told you.[33]

According to the Crown, this letter was

> important, as it showed his frame of mind on that night. On our submission it is a letter of farewell and indicated that the writer intended to do away with himself. It showed that the outlook was bleak enough for him and after straightening out the affairs of Betty nothing mattered.[34]

Between half-past-seven and eight o'clock that evening Stark arrived at the house. Thelma was taking a bath. According to Stark, Thelma

> sang out to me 'Oh, I won't be a minute'. While I was waiting I had a conversation with Mareo. He told me that Thelma thought she was pregnant, that he had bought some medicine for her, just to show her that he was looking after her. He told me that the chemist wanted to charge him – I'm not sure if it was £2/10 or £3 – for the medicine and he told the chemist that he couldn't afford it, because he was Mareo from the St. James orchestra. Because he was out of work. The chemist had said 'If that is the case I will let you have it for £1. When he was talking of her thinking she was pregnant he said 'She is silly. She is only four days overdue, and in any case it is impossible.'[35]

While Mareo and Freda were talking, Thelma was still in the bath. After finishing her bath she and Freda went into her bedroom. According to Stark, Thelma did some 'leg exercises', Mareo came into the room, and Thelma took some of the medicine that Mareo had just purchased from the chemist. Thelma asked Stark to come and stay the weekend and Mareo asked her to arrive early because he would later be 'out on business'.[36] Having promised to return the next day, Stark left and the Mareos went to bed. According to Mareo, Thelma slept in the double bed and he in the chair next to her 'in case she wanted me'. He justified this unusual sleeping arrangement by claiming that '[a]ll my married life to her, if I came home from the theatre and found her drunk, I let her sleep on the bed while I myself slept on a sofa in the dining room'.[37]

Saturday

Upon awakening on the Saturday morning, Mareo found that Thelma 'still appeared in a drunken sleep and [he] did not wake her up'.[38] Mareo then took a bath. Thelma must have risen from bed because Mareo's son, Graham, testified that he heard a 'couple of bumps' and went into his stepmother's room to find her 'swaying' in her dressing gown, 'clutching the dressing table drawer' and saying 'something about some curry' that 'didn't make sense'. Graham called out to his father and they both put Thelma back to bed where she soon fell asleep.[39] Mareo then left the house on business to return at about 1.00 p.m. Graham was at home during this period looking after his stepmother except for some time after 11.30 a.m. when he left the house. Thelma was still in bed when Graham left.

As she had promised the previous evening, Stark returned to the house at about 3.00 or 3.30 p.m. on Saturday. It is not entirely clear what happened after Stark's return because her account differed significantly from that given by Mareo and Graham. However, since the Crown's case depended largely on Stark's evidence we will, at least for the moment, stick to her version.

According to Stark, Mareo and Thelma were in the bedroom when she arrived. She did not see either of them until 'about half past five' when Mareo emerged from the bedroom to go to the bathroom. He was, she testified, 'very unsteady on his feet and lurched once against the wall', but she did not smell anything on his breath. In the passage Mareo told Stark about the events of the day and she then went into the bedroom to see Thelma, who was 'fast asleep' and 'breathing as though she was in a heavy sleep'. A little later she asked Mareo whether they should call a doctor and '[h]e said oh, it couldn't hurt her to sleep a little longer, but if she wasn't awake soon he would send for one. He said he couldn't get a doctor or he would get into trouble for getting her the medicine that she had had [for her overdue period]'.[40]

Mareo, Graham and Freda then had tea. Afterwards, Stark checked to see if Thelma was awake and Mareo received a phone call from Eleanor Brownlee asking him if he wanted to go out for a drive. 'That's just what I need, a blow in the fresh air', he told Stark; '[i]f Thelma should wake, tell her I have gone out on business.'[41] Just before leaving, Stark asked him again if he should call a doctor, and he said he would if she wasn't awake by the time he got home.

Half an hour after Mareo left, Stark was in the sitting room and heard her name called. She went and said, '"What do you want, Thelma?"and she said "Freda, I heard your voice". She was awake but she seemed as though she had been in a very heavy sleep and was dazed. Her eyelids were very heavy and her speech wasn't distinct.'[42] Mareo returned about half an hour later at approximately ten o'clock and Stark suggested to him that they try Thelma on some smelling salts. Mareo and Freda managed to support Thelma in a sitting position and give her a drink of water.

Graham then went to a place called the All Night Pharmacy for smelling salts or sal volatile. While he was gone Stark and Mareo 'told her funny stories to keep her awake. They were funny stories and limericks. She knew what they were because she laughed.'[43] About half an hour later Graham returned and Freda gave Thelma three doses of sal volatile. Recovering somewhat, Thelma chewed a toffee given to her by Mareo and they then played a game which involved Thelma looking at all the objects in the room and naming them: 'She started off with the dressing table and chair and then she closed her eyes. Mr Mareo said "Open your eyes and look at them" so she opened her eyes and started off again to name them. She named them.'[44]

Soon after this game, Mareo and Graham left the room. Stark's account of what happened next needs to be given almost in full because according to the Crown this was when Mareo murdered his wife:

[Graham] brought in a cup of hot milk and gave it to me. He went out again then. He brought in another cup for himself. I did not want the milk. I didn't drink it. . . . Graham threw the milk that was brought for me out the window. . . . Mr Mareo came into the room next. He brought a cup of hot milk in with him and a plate with a slice of dry bread. I was sitting on the bed then, with Thelma. At that time I had let her lie back on the pillow. When Mareo came in with the milk and bread we sat her up in bed again and first of all Mr Mareo broke off a piece of dry bread and gave it to her. She was chewing it rather slowly so I said to him I thought it would be rather doughy for her to eat. She chewed the mouthful that she had and swallowed it. I then gave her a drink of the milk. I held it in my own hand and she drank not quite half a cup. She wasn't capable of holding it herself. Then I spilt some of it round her nightgown so I handed it to Graham to see if he could do better. When I gave her half the cup she did not do anything then. When Graham had given her some more from the cup he handed the cup back to me again. Then when I was giving her the last lot she was getting very drowsy and she closed her teeth and wouldn't have any more. This was given to her from the cup direct. No spoon was used.

Just before we gave her the milk she said she wanted to go to the lavatory. After she started going off to sleep – after I had given her the milk – so I thought I had better take her out before she went right off to sleep. So I asked Mr Mareo to help me to take her outside. He did not do so. He couldn't stand on his feet very well – he fell across the bed, so I asked Graham to help me take her out. Graham and I got her out of bed and put one arm round our shoulders and our arms round her back so as to support her. We sat her on the bed first and then put her arms around us. She wasn't capable of walking on her feet – she was dragging them, so we practically had to carry her out.

When we got to the lavatory I went inside with her. . . . Mrs Mareo used the lavatory. . . . By the time I got Graham to help me back with her she had fallen fast asleep. She was taken back to her room in the same way that we had taken her from it. We were away from the room altogether not more than ten minutes. . . .

When we were taking her out I did not notice any odour from her breath. No smell of alcohol. . . .

When we got back to the room Graham and myself put her back to bed. She just lay back on the pillows. She was asleep by then.[45]

According to the Crown, while Mareo had been in the kitchen heating the milk he had deliberately laced it with a lethal dose of veronal.

Incidentally, in his final address to the jury, Johnstone (the Crown Prosecutor at the first trial) did maintain that he had 'proved conclusively' that Mareo also administered veronal to

Thelma on the Friday night as well, but for a number of reasons the Crown's case focused almost exclusively on the Saturday night and the cup of milk. Two members of *The Duchess of Danzig* cast, Mrs Freda Evans and Miss Doris Bransgrove, testified that they had read about Thelma's death in the newspaper on the following Tuesday and had decided to visit Mareo together that day to offer their sympathy. Both women told the court that during this visit Mareo told them that he had given Thelma veronal on the Friday night. However neither Mareo nor any other witness could confirm that he had either given Thelma veronal or said that he had. Moreover under cross-examination by the Defence both Mrs Evans and Miss Bransgrove revealed that they were close friends and neighbours, that they both disliked Mareo and admired Thelma, and that they had not thought to tell the authorities about their 'sympathy' visit until the police visited them more than a month later. Mareo's counsel, O'Leary, asked Mrs Evans whether theirs had been 'the visit of two curious women' and she replied rather unconvincingly '[n]ot necessarily . . . We went to see Mr Mareo in his time of grief. – Q. The man you didn't like? – No'.[46] However, even if these two women were to be believed, it was plain that administering a sleeping draught such as veronal to a mildly unwell woman was quite a different matter to giving an apparently very sick woman barely capable of staying awake the same drug disguised in a cup of milk. While the second action might well be murder, the first might be at best (or worst) manslaughter. Besides, only the second of these actions had been witnessed by anyone other than the accused and the deceased. Thus while the Crown maintained that Mareo had given Thelma veronal on at least two occasions, proof of the murder charge largely depended on Stark's testimony cited above and the logical inferences that could be drawn from it.

After Thelma was assisted back from the lavatory, Stark said she told Mareo they should call a doctor but 'Mareo said that a few hours sleep wouldn't hurt her and it wouldn't hurt her to sleep until morning'.[47] The whole household went to sleep, Freda in bed with Thelma and Mareo in a chair beside them. Stark said that she could not sleep that evening and that she heard Thelma 'breathing very heavily' and making a 'gurgling sound in her throat'. She called Mareo for assistance but could not rouse him. Nevertheless Stark, who was worried that Thelma 'was going to be sick', managed to sit her up in bed even though she remained asleep.[48]

Sunday and Monday

The next morning, when all but Thelma had woken up, Mareo left the house for a ten o'clock appointment. Just before he left Stark said she asked him 'don't you think we had better get a doctor. Thelma has been asleep practically two days' and he replied '[i]f she is not awake by the time I get home I will call a doctor then. A couple of hours more won't hurt her'. Mareo returned at about one o'clock and Stark told him, 'Thelma isn't awake yet, and I think you had better get a doctor straight away.' His response according to her was 'Oh, it's all right. I rang up the chemist, and he said that the sleep was due to nervous exhaustion, and that Thelma could sleep for two or three days, without any ill effect, and that she would wake up feeling very weak but wanting food'. Stark insisted that 'Thelma's breathing very heavily' but Mareo thought that 'that's just the way you have her lying – on her back' and so they shifted her onto her side.[49]

The rest of the afternoon Stark attended to the comatose Thelma while Mareo slept in a chair beside the bed. At around six o'clock Graham, Stark and Mareo had tea and at about seven o'clock Stark prepared to leave. When she was ready she told Mareo that 'Thelma has been sleeping nearly three days and I really think she should have a doctor'.[50] Mareo promised to call a doctor if she did not wake up in the next few hours and Graham accompanied Stark back to her house.

On Monday morning Stark called Graham. Then at one o'clock Graham rang her and she went straight out to the house:

I met Mr Mareo first when I went out. He said 'Go in and see her'. I did. She was in a terrible condition. She was blue in the face, and perspiration had dried on her face, and there was some brown saliva that had run down her face and caked in her hair. She was just gasping for breath. I said to Mareo 'Oh, why didn't you get a doctor', and with that I ran out to ring up from Mrs Knight's next door. I didn't wait to hear any reply from Mareo before I went. . . .

After having rung him [the doctor] I went back to the house. I went into the bedroom where Thelma was. Mr Mareo suggested that I should wash her. I did so. When I had done so the doctor called – Dr. Dreadon. He got there about three o'clock. While I was washing Mrs Mareo the accused did not assist me. After I had washed her he came in and helped me to put on a clean nightgown. When I was doing that I noticed the sheets were wet and had bloodstains on them. Mareo and I came to a conclusion about the stains. He said she had just come on unwell. I thought that too. We moved her onto the clean side of the bed. Then Dr. Dreadon arrived. . . . Dr. Dreadon looked at her and opened her eyes and he said 'Oh, it looks like veronal poisoning'. He asked accused if there was any of it in the house. Accused said 'Yes'. He said he had been taking it to make him sleep. He said that he kept it outside – I think it was in a suitcase – outside in the washhouse. I said to him to go out and see if any had been taken. He went out and came back with an empty bottle. He showed it to the doctor and said that it had been practically full.[51]

Dr Dreadon then called an ambulance. Despite treatment at the hospital, Thelma died about two hours after her admission.

Soon afterwards, Eleanor Brownlee drove Mareo at his request to a telephone so he could inform a number of people of the news, then to the *Herald* office to make a death announcement, the undertakers, and the Clarendon Hotel for liquor. About an hour and a half later they returned to Tenterden Avenue where they met Stark, Graham and the detectives. Mareo told one of the detectives, 'I have had a double whiskey and I have a bottle of brandy in the car to make me sleep tonight. I feel like doing myself in.'[52] When asked by Detective Meiklejohn how his wife came to have so much veronal, Mareo replied, 'Do you think I am a murderer?' Questioned about his own veronal consumption, Mareo also asked, 'Do I look like a drug addict?'[53] Detective Meiklejohn then brought Stark into the room and he said to Mareo

> 'Miss Stark has stated that she asked you to call a doctor for your wife several times'. [Mareo] said, 'I don't remember that, my dear'. . . . .
>
> I mentioned about the bottle of dope [the medicine purchased from the chemist because of Thelma's concern about her overdue period].
>
> I said 'Miss Stark has stated that you told her you had bought a bottle of dope from the chemist for your wife' and he [Mareo] said [to Stark], 'You are mistaken, my dear.'[54]

After this conversation, Mareo took the detectives out to the washhouse to show them the empty veronal bottle. Handing over the bottle to Detective Meiklejohn, Mareo confessed, 'I feel like a criminal.' On top of the suitcase containing the empty veronal bottle were three empty whisky bottles and an empty pill box from which, according to Stark, Thelma had taken the medicine purchased from the chemist when her period was overdue. Mareo identified this as 'the box I got the veronal tablets in', but he could not account for how it had got there. They all then went back to the front room of the house where Mareo read his first statement in which he referred to Thelma's drinking and he said, 'I feel like a cad saying all this about my wife but I've got to protect myself.' He also asked the detectives, 'Is there anything in this to hang me' and confessed, 'I feel like going and hanging myself, bringing all this veronal into the house.'[55]

Tuesday and Later

Eleanor Brownlee left Tenterden Avenue at about eleven o'clock on Monday evening. According to her, Mareo and Graham arrived uninvited and unannounced at her rented room at about half past two the next morning where Graham slept on the bed and she and Mareo in chairs. The next day they went back to Tenterden Avenue. That morning Stark claimed she received a phone call from Mareo in which

> [h]e said that he knew how I felt over Thelma's death – he knew how much I would miss her, and he would miss her too. And he told me to stop crying, or he would be crying too. Then he said 'Fritters dear, you'll have to be careful what you say to the detectives or you'll have a rope around my neck'. And he said 'The next time you give a statement tell them that you weren't in a fit state when you gave your first statement.'[56]

The same day Mrs Evans and Miss Bransgrove made their visit and Mareo told them that he was going to take a veronal tablet and have a good sleep. Mrs Evans testified that she said

> 'Surely you won't take a veronal tablet when you know the way Thelma suffered' and he said 'Thelma suffered no pain.' He said he hadn't got a doctor before because he was so used to seeing Thelma 'Canned'. We left shortly after. Just before we rose Mr Mareo said he was really frightened and would we help him if he needed us. Then as we were leaving he grasped the arm of Miss Bransgrove and myself and said 'They won't hang me will they?' When we arrived there – before he said 'Thank God she wasn't insured', he said that Graham and himself had walked the streets all night.[57]

Eleanor Brownlee stayed with Mareo and Graham at Tenterden Avenue for two days after Thelma's death. A few days later Mareo and Graham moved out of Tenterden Avenue and went to a flat in Waterloo Quadrant where Brownlee often visited. She and Mareo continued to work on a scenario for the film Mareo was planning make. According to the *Herald*'s summary of the Crown's closing address

> As soon as Mrs Mareo died, Miss Brownlee was installed at No. 1 Tenterden Avenue for as long as Mareo remained there,

and later her room at Wyndham Street was constantly at his disposal – all this without any fee save the expectation of a problematical return from a film production.[58]

The detectives returned to Tenterden Avenue for the last time on 19 April, Good Friday. An inquest into Thelma's death had been held a few days earlier on the Tuesday at which Betty had testified that Thelma drank excessively. This had been reported in the *Auckland Star* and on Good Friday Detective Meiklejohn 'commented to accused that it was a pity that she said what she did. I said people were commenting and saying that she did not drink as much as what was said. Accused agreed that that was correct.' Betty then came into the room and kissed and hugged her father while he said

'You will visit me at the prison, won't you Betty?' She said 'Of course, Daddy.' Mareo then said, 'Why did you say all that about poor Thelma'. He said that to Betty. She said 'They told me I had to, and I did it to protect you, daddy'. He commented that she should not have said so much.[59]

After the detectives had left Betty later confessed in court that she

did something in relation to the bottles there that afternoon. I took off two labels and threw them away or burnt them. One bottle was like a small aspirin bottle. I think the label had on it 'Barbitone' or something like that. I took that label off and burnt it. I am not sure what I did with it – I threw it away somewhere. I don't know what the other bottle was – a sort of medicine bottle. It had on it some sort of red label I think. I did the same with that label as the other. I threw the bottles out. I did this because I knew that veronal had been found in the house and I thought the chemist would get in for a row. You are not supposed to buy that stuff and I threw the labels away because I thought the chemist would get in for a row. Mareo was out of the house that Friday. I don't think he was in the room when I did that.[60]

The police later found these bottles in the backyard as well as the remains of an insurance policy in the name of 'Thelma'.

The detectives visited Mareo at his new address and Brownlee's place on several other occasions, finally reading Mareo the warrant for his arrest nearly five months after Thelma's death, on 2 September 1935. Mareo responded, 'Really, on what evidence, this is ridiculous. What evidence have you got?'[61]

The only other evidence relevant to the Crown's case was the report of the government analyst who examined portions of Thelma's body as well as her mattress and bedding, and the coroner's report on the post-mortem examination carried out the day after her death. According to the coroner, Dr Walter Gilmour, a pathologist at Auckland Hospital, Thelma died of uncomplicated veronal poisoning, 'probably' from a dose of 'at least 100 gr'.[62] Dr Gilmour thought that Thelma had one dose of veronal on either the Friday night or the Saturday morning and the fatal dose on the Saturday night because it was impossible for a patient to awaken from a comatose state and then relapse into a fatal coma. On the evidence of Stark and Graham, Dr Gilmour thought that Thelma was not in a coma when she drank the milk and would have fully recovered if she had not taken or been given another dose. During the trial two other doctors with limited experience in the treatment of veronal poisoning were called to give evidence. They both confirmed Dr Gilmour's conclusions.

Thus the Crown's case was reasonably straightforward. While Thelma was recovering from at least one poisonous dose of veronal, Mareo contrived the administration of a fatal dose disguised in a cup of milk so that he might replace his wife with his mistress, Eleanor Brownlee. '[T]he possibility of a third finding' other than murder or not guilty of murder, manslaughter, was, the Crown argued, 'not here'.[63]

CHAPTER TWO

'Canned': Mareo's Defence

MAREO DID NOT TAKE the witness stand during the trial. According to his junior counsel, (later Sir) Trevor Henry, this was in large part because he could remember very little about the events of the fatal weekend. In light of that fact, it appears that Mareo's senior counsel, Humphrey O'Leary KC, decided to take advantage of the procedural rule that permitted him to address the jury last where no Defence witnesses were called. O'Leary's decision to call neither Mareo nor any other witnesses perhaps indicates his assessment of the strength (or rather weakness) of the Crown's case. O'Leary's strategy seems to have been to attempt to raise doubts about Mareo's alleged motive, the Crown's interpretation of his guilty behaviour, and the scientific veracity of the Crown's medical witnesses. He also attempted to present a plausible alternative explanation of Thelma's death.

Mareo's Motive

In his final address to the jury, Johnstone maintained that although the Crown had shown that 'the accused had tired of his wife' the jury were 'not bound to assign any motive'.[1] Yet, while it is true that the Crown does not need to prove motive, it may logically have some bearing on the question of whether the accused intended to kill (which is murder) or was reckless as to the consequences of his or her actions (which is manslaughter). It is easier to prove that an accused intended the consequences of certain actions if they can also show that he or she had some kind of motive for achieving those consequences.

However, even the Prosecution seems to have been confused about Mareo's possible intentions on the weekend in question.

As we have seen, they argued that the letter Mareo gave Betty revealing that he was not her 'legal' father demonstrated that he 'intended to do away with himself'. But why would a man intending such an action also be planning *at the same time* to murder his wife and replace her with his mistress for financial gain? It is possible that Mareo could have been both suicidal and coldly plotting his wife's death, but this seems rather unlikely.

Yet, even if he had not been intending suicide, the nature of his relationship with Eleanor Brownlee remained unclear. Both Brownlee and Mareo firmly denied that they were having an affair, the latter, according to Stark, rather unkindly telling his wife that 'he couldn't possibly be in love with Eleanor as she had no personality and looks'.[2] Stark also testified that Thelma had objected to Brownlee doing some of Mareo's washing and cleaning his room at the theatre but Mareo maintained to the police that Thelma had said about the washing '"[o]n second thoughts I think it will save me a lot of trouble" or words to that effect and there the matter ended'.[3] Brownlee even said that on the first occasion Thelma had actually asked her to clean Mareo's ties and evening vest since she did not understand how to use starch.

Of course there was the bathroom incident after which Brownlee had written at Mareo's request:

> Dear Thelma,
> Mr Mareo told me tonight that you are still upset over what occurred on Saturday evening. I am very sorry if I was partly the cause of your distress. May I assure you that if I appeared to intrude it certainly was quite unintentional, and I very much regret having caused you any annoyance.
> Believe me, yours sincerely,
> Eleanor J. Brownlee[4]

It is telling that Brownlee only apologised for intruding into a domestic dispute and did not feel it necessary even to allude to any suspicion of an affair between herself and Mareo. Indeed, O'Leary maintained that when Stark and Thelma left the house after this dispute 'the presence of Miss Brownlee there was just an excuse'. According to the *Herald*'s summary, '[h]is Honor interposed to say there was no evidence to bear out that suggestion. The evidence showed, on the contrary, that the cause of the quarrel was Miss Brownlee's going into the bathroom'.[5] However, this assertion of Mr Justice Fair's does not precisely accord with the evidence of either Stark or Brownlee. According to Stark, Thelma initially said that Eleanor could not stay the night because, presumably, 'Freda was staying here' to which Mareo responded, 'Oh, she can sleep anywhere.'[6] Thus Thelma's initial problem with Brownlee was that she would inconvenience their sleeping arrangements. And, according to Brownlee (whose account differs significantly from Stark's), she only went into the bathroom *after* she had heard Thelma call out hysterically.

In reality the only evidence that Mareo and Brownlee were having an affair was the fact that they spent so much time together. Yet while it was rare for men and women to work so closely together during the 1930s, at least as equals, some workplaces – such as theatres – were obvious exceptions. On the vast majority of occasions, Mareo and Brownlee were simply working together, either on the scenario for the film or on theatre business. They had first met because of Brownlee's desire to learn orchestration, and she had initially paid Mareo for his tuition. No one ever suggested that they met in secret, and after Thelma's death they still continued to meet openly. Mareo and Brownlee might have thought that the best way of keeping their affair secret was to conduct it as publicly as possible. Yet, while in one of Edgar Allan Poe's stories a character conceals a letter by using it to visibly plug a hole in a wall, it is rather unlikely that they would have chosen to conceal their relationship in such a manner. Betty's response to O'Leary's inquiry about noticing 'any signs of undue relationship between Mareo and Eleanor Brownlee' seems spontaneous and therefore probably reliable: 'Good heavens, No.'[7]

Of course there is nothing in the trial that definitely rules out the possibility that Brownlee was in love with Mareo and that he knew it. Since Brownlee was the daughter of well-off Aucklanders, it might have been that the bankrupt and unemployed Mareo was anticipating a large dowry. Nevertheless, it is a courageous or extremely desperate man who would risk being hanged on the assumption not only that a woman seventeen years his junior would marry him, but also that her parents would approve of the marriage and dispense with some of their fortune accordingly.

Besides, Stark's evidence that the Mareos' marriage was all but over was contradicted by other testimony. Some degree of tension or conflict in their marriage was only to be expected: both were out of work, one was visiting a doctor for a nervous condition, the other drinking heavily and taking veronal, and they were living in an unusual household. Mareo's daughter and son were respectively only eight years and twelve years younger than their stepmother. Thelma and Betty did not get on because Thelma objected to Betty doing the housework and usurping her position as 'mistress of the house'. Thelma's 'bosom friend' had taken up almost semi-permanent residence and there were often, according to Betty, other 'theatricals in the house when the shows were on'.[8] In their different ways, both Mareo and Thelma would have been difficult to live with. Thus it is not surprising that they quarrelled. However, Graham could only remember his father and stepmother quarrelling on two occasions and on both of these they were drunk. Stark even told the court that after Thelma had gone to see Dr Walton, Mareo

> and his wife seemed to be getting on quite all right. The weekend before she died I went out on the Saturday night and we played cards – that was the Saturday night, it would be 6th April. Mr Mareo, Thelma, Graham and I were there. We played cards.[9]

Later Stark would also remember that Mareo had been teaching them all German.

In addition Mareo stood to lose something by replacing his wife with Brownlee. On the weekend of Thelma's death, Brownlee was writing a letter on behalf of Mareo to the J.C. Williamson Theatre Company in Australia proposing that they fund a light opera company in which Thelma would be the leading lady. Mareo was also promoting his film scenario to potential financiers on the basis that she would be its main star. As O'Leary pointed out to the jury, Thelma 'was a necessity to him if his programme was to be carried out. What use would Eleanor Brownlee, not suited for the stage, have been to him in this connection? Thelma, on the other hand, was essential for the work.'[10]

Mareo's Guilty Behaviour

Perhaps the most telling aspect of Mareo's guilty behaviour was his apparent repeated reluctance to call a doctor. The Attorney-General at the time of the trials, Mason, would later claim that this was the 'hub' of the case.[11] However, while such behaviour might be seen as irresponsible and even reprehensible, it does not indicate that Mareo was a murderer. The jury would have had to reject two possible explanations for his delay: that he was used to seeing Thelma 'Canned', and that he was concerned about the nature of the medicine he had purchased from the chemist because of Thelma's anxiety about her delayed period. The first of these explanations is quite plausible (as we shall soon see), and the second not only accounts for his reluctance to call a doctor but goes some way towards proving his innocence.

Because Thelma had her period while still in a coma, her fears about being pregnant had been unfounded. Furthermore, as we have also seen, Mareo believed that Thelma could not have been pregnant and the chemist who supplied him with the drugs concerned, David Morgan, testified that he had told him that 'his wife was slightly overdue and wanted a corrective mixture'. Morgan supplied him with a mixture described as 'a general tonic' to correct 'general debility' and 'satisfy the mind' suitable for both men and women. The 'corrective mixture' was not, Morgan testified, an abortifacient. Morgan also supplied Mareo with some apparently harmless Burroughs-Wellcome Varium tablets.[12]

However, at a time when the penalty for administering an abortifacient was life imprisonment, a man expressing concern about his wife's delayed period might either be misconstrued or he might subsequently believe that he had been misconstrued. In some circumstances it might have been difficult to tell whether an understandably vague husband was requesting a medicine to calm his wife's nerves and therefore induce her period or whether he was asking for an abortifacient. Significantly, Morgan contradicted Mareo's story that he had initially charged him '£2/10 – or £3', but agreed to let him have the medicines for £1 because he was out of work. The price of the medicines, according to Morgan, was only '5/- or 6/-'.[13] Assuming that Stark's testimony is accurate and Mareo had no discernible motive to inflate greatly the price of the medicines (because that would make them appear more likely to be abortifacients), why would Morgan lie? Presumably, he either did not want to appear as the kind of man who charged exorbitant prices for placebos or did not want anybody to know that the reason why one of the drugs was so expensive was that it was an abortifacient.

It is likely, then, that Mareo believed that Morgan had misinterpreted his request and supplied him with an abortifacient. When he visited the Mareos at home, Dr Dreadon testified that Mareo had told him that Thelma 'had taken some medicine three days previously – he said that she had been several days overdue with her menstrual periods and thought she was pregnant and she had taken this medicine to try and put it right'.[14] And according to the resident doctor at the hospital, Dr Keenan, Mareo had said

> that Thelma his wife had a horror of pregnancy, that she had obtained some medicine from a chemist and he had thought her condition was due to the taking of this medicine. He made it quite clear who had obtained the medicine from the chemist – that she had.[15]

Dr Keenan had then sent Mareo to have his blood tested. According to him Mareo 'expressed every willingness to give blood for his wife – to do everything that was possible'. In short, Mareo behaved as though he wanted the doctors to guess the nature of Morgan's drugs in order that they might save her life, but as though he feared prosecution for administering an abortifacient.

After Thelma's death some time probably passed before its cause was confirmed. Although the government analyst received portions of her body the day after her death, he was still receiving parts of her bedding (in which veronal from her urine was present) about six weeks later. Immediately after listing the dates on which he received various 'exhibits', the government analyst testified that 'I examined the organs for poison' which seems to imply that he did not begin his analysis until all the 'exhibits' had been received.[16] Immediately after Thelma's death Dr Gilmour did conduct a post-mortem examination but he did not testify as to whether he came to the conclusion that Thelma had died of veronal poisoning. In court he testified that he had 'heard the evidence given by Kenneth Massy Griffin [the government analyst]. Having heard that evidence I come to the conclusion that death was due to veronal poisoning'.[17] This implies that he was unable to ascertain the cause of death without Griffin's analysis. In other words, it may not have been until *after* Mareo had given his various statements to the police that the cause of Thelma's death was confirmed.

Certainly on the evidence of his lies about Morgan's drugs, it seems that Mareo was uncertain as to the cause of her death. Significantly, before her death he lied to the doctors only about who had purchased the drugs from Morgan. However, after Thelma's death Mareo denied to the police on several occasions not only having purchased this medicine but also even being aware that his wife had taken it just before she died. Presumably, he feared that he would now be charged with killing his wife with an abortifacient.

Mareo's confessions about the veronal confirm this interpretation. Dr Dreadon testified that Mareo immediately denied that Thelma took 'dope' of any kind, confessed to taking veronal himself and willingly fetched the bottle in which he kept his supply. According to Dr Dreadon, Mareo seemed 'genuinely surprised' when he discovered that the veronal bottle was empty.[18] He was just as forthcoming to Dr Keenan at the hospital and later he gave long and detailed accounts of all his veronal purchases and his consumption habits to the police on several occasions. The only time he was ever evasive about the veronal or behaved in a guilty fashion was in revealing the names of the chemists from whom he had purchased the drug. However, this can be explained by the fact that sale of the drug had been restricted a couple of weeks earlier, and Mareo was concerned that he would get these chemists into trouble for selling a drug illegally. Thus, when he took the detectives out to the washhouse to show them the empty veronal bottle, Mareo exclaimed, 'Oh, you'll get the chemist's name from this,' and, 'Oh, please don't take it.'[19] When the police asked him a few days after Thelma's death where he had purchased the veronal, reassuring him that '[w]e are not concerned with prosecuting a chemist for any offence', Mareo replied, 'I will if asked to do so on oath.'[20] Furthermore, as O'Leary pointed out to the jury,

> [Mareo] went to chemists who knew him, and the purchases he made could be easily ascertained . . . Was that the action of a guilty man? Would he not have gone to the 80 or 90 chemists in Auckland who did not know him?[21]

Yet despite such apparently compelling evidence that Mareo had not poisoned his wife with veronal, there was a crucial problem with O'Leary's case. According to the *Herald*'s account – on which we have in part to rely since transcripts of the final addresses to the juries either were not made or do not survive – O'Leary told the first jury that '[t]he reason Mareo did not get a doctor earlier was the reason he had given, that he had given her medicine to prevent childbirth'. This would indicate that O'Leary believed that Mareo had asked Morgan for an abortifacient. However, in the same address, O'Leary had said that 'instead of letting her continue to *fear* childbirth and possibly destroy herself, Mareo went and got medicine to save her from this *fear*' [our emphasis], the implication being that the medicines were merely for her mental condition or possibly to induce her period.[22]

Similarly, as we shall see, O'Leary was vague about Mareo's lesbian accusation. O'Leary could have said that Mareo was lying about his wife's sexual preferences because he felt guilty about giving her an abortifacient. If he could convince people that his wife was a lesbian then it would be unlikely that anyone would believe that she would be in need of an abortifacient. However, if O'Leary had argued that Mareo was lying, this would have played into the hands of the Crown who made much of the fact that he was the kind of man prepared to 'blacken' his wife's name in order to save his own skin. Besides O'Leary had reminded the court that the senior detective involved in the case had testified that when Mareo told the police that his 'wife was fonder of women than of men' he had also demanded, 'I don't want this to go down.'[23] His 'accusation' was in fact only recorded in a much later statement after police had questioned him about this off-the-record statement. Moreover, while he probably did repeat both the lesbian and alcholic charges after Thelma's death in order to exonerate himself, Mareo had first made these charges, according to Dr Walton and Stark's testimony, not only *before* Thelma's death but *before* he could reasonably have been expected to have formulated any plan to murder her.

Alternatively, however, if O'Leary had argued that Thelma really was a lesbian, then he would have seriously damaged his case that Mareo felt guilty about Morgan's drugs not the veronal. O'Leary was caught on the horns of a dilemma. It seems that rather than attempting to resolve it, he chose to fudge things. This may have been because his analytical skills were not up to the task or, as we think more likely, because of his attitudes towards women. Although O'Leary was one of the leading criminal barristers of his day (he is reputed never to have lost a jury trial in his first nine years of regular criminal practice), and in 1946 was appointed Chief Justice, it was later noted by another Chief Justice that '[f]or such a personable man he was curiously shy of women (it is doubtful if he ever employed a woman typist) but he loved the company of men and, best, his fellow lawyers of all ages'.[24] A case concerned so much with the intimate physical and sexual lives of two women was perhaps not ideal for such a man.

The Medical Evidence

The only facts not disputed by O'Leary were: (1) that Mareo had purchased the veronal that (2) killed Thelma. At issue was whether he had administered the veronal to her and, if he had, whether this had been done either recklessly or with murderous intent. Unlike the infamous *Munn* trial of 1930, where the accused was charged with and convicted of murdering his wife with strychnine, an obvious obstacle the Prosecution had in Mareo's case was that veronal was a medicinal drug which Thelma might have come to take herself in any number of ways. As the prominent Auckland prosecutor Vincent Meredith (who was later to become involved in the case) was to point out in another context, it was extremely difficult to prove that someone had been murdered with veronal because 'veronal could be bought freely [at least before 1 April 1935] and it was impossible to establish that the deceased had not himself had veronal and self-administered it'.[25] Indeed, in 1933 there had been another famous criminal trial in Auckland where a nurse, Elspeth Kerr (who would today be a clear candidate for a diagnosis of Munchausen's Syndrome by Proxy), was accused of attempting to murder her adopted daughter with veronal. Although there was clear evidence that the only way in which the child could have taken veronal was through the auspices of her mother, the juries in Kerr's first two trials could not agree. It was only after she had endured a third trial that she was convicted of attempted murder. Although after investigations by the real-life prototype of Georges Simenon's fictional Inspector Maigret, the young Parisian woman Violette Noziere, who killed her father with veronal in 1934 (after he had lain in a coma for about thirty hours), was convicted of murder and sentenced to the guillotine, no one living under British law had ever been convicted of murdering someone with veronal. Thus O'Leary (who was unlikely to have known of the Noziere case) could inform the jury that 'a conviction of murder . . . would make history'.[26]

As far as the medical evidence was concerned, there were three main questions.

Firstly, how much veronal had Thelma consumed over the weekend? This was crucial because O'Leary raised the possibility that Thelma might have been 'susceptible' to the drug and therefore killed by a relatively 'normal' dose. Obviously, it is unlikely that a man such as Mareo, used to taking the drug frequently, could have intended to murder her with a 'normal' dose. One of the Crown's three doctors, Dr Gunson, denied that Thelma displayed the symptoms of a 'susceptible' patient suffering from veronal poisoning, but he neither explained why a normal dose for a susceptible person did not produce the same symptoms as an overdose for a normal person, nor described how susceptible patients behaved after they had taken a medicinal dose.[27] Nevertheless, on the authority of the overseas expert toxicologist, Sir William Willcox, all three doctors agreed that Thelma had taken a total of about 100 grains of veronal. The authority of Sir William was crucial because Thelma's body did not contain all the veronal, unknown amounts having been excreted in her urine both before her final period of sleep and later on a nightdress that had been washed either by Stark (according to Brownlee) or by Brownlee (according to Stark). However, O'Leary was able to point out to the doctor who had conducted the post-mortem, Dr Gilmour, that

> Sir W. Willcox was unable to say how much veronal was taken in those cases [of veronal poisoning to which Dr. Gilmour had been referring] – It isn't recorded [conceded Gilmour]. Q. If it had been obtained it would have been recorded? – In one case he says 'probably about 100 gr. were taken' . . . Q. That is the only case in which there is an estimate of the amount taken? – The only fatal case in this series.[28]

Somewhat later Dr Gunson also admitted that he could not say why Sir William had estimated the amount of veronal in only one fatal case. Clearly, the Crown's doctors were considerably more certain than the authority upon whom they relied.

Secondly, how much veronal was in the milk and was it the fatal dose? As we have seen, Stark testified that Thelma drank at least half the cup of milk without the aid of a spoon. In contrast, Graham claimed that Thelma did not drink directly from the cup and drank '[o]nly a very little' from several attempts to give her the milk from a spoon.[29] Since a few spoonfuls of milk could not have contained a fatal amount of veronal (due to its lack of solubility), Thelma could not have been given a fatal dose if Graham's testimony is to be believed. Thus Dr Gilmour testified that at the preliminary inquiry he had formed the opinion on the basis only of Graham's evidence that it was 'impossible to say' that the last dose of veronal was in the milk. O'Leary then asked:

> In this Court you are in the same position with regard to the evidence except that you read Graham Mareo's evidence? – Yes. Q. Are you in any better position to form an opinion as to whether the last dose was taken in the milk? – No. Q. Worse I suggest? – Yes, possibly. Q. Why worse? – Based on the estimate of the quantity of milk taken.[30]

Thirdly, was any veronal in the milk at all? The evidence that it was in the milk was completely circumstantial and therefore based on the principle allegedly derived from Sir William Willcox that someone could not relapse back into a coma without a further dose of veronal. However, according to Dr Ludbrook, Thelma was not even initially in a coma but 'sleeping naturally', albeit from what O'Leary described and he agreed was a 'slight overdose of veronal'.[31] But even if she had initially been in a coma, it is by no means clear that she ever came out of this coma before taking the milk. O'Leary had discovered a case of veronal poisoning documented by a Dr Durrant in which a man had roused from an apparent coma, been able to take liquids only by a teaspoon, and then relapsed back into a coma from which he never recovered. Dr Gilmour maintained that this case did not apply to Thelma's because '[h]e could be roused by effort – but not of his own accord'.[32] However, Thelma only roused of her own accord according to Stark's evidence. Although Stark testified that Thelma had called out just before Graham went to the Dispensary for the sal volatile, Graham said, 'I didn't hear her.'[33] Stark maintained that Thelma chewed and swallowed the bread whereas Graham remembered that '[t]hey forced a bit in between her teeth but I don't know if she swallowed it'.[34] Furthermore there was the following exchange between O'Leary and Graham:

> During the time that you were giving her the milk wasn't it that she was just trying to go off to sleep – Yes. Q. And she had to be roused when the attempt was made? – Yes. Q. She couldn't sit up herself and take it? – No.[35]

But the really telling evidence that veronal may not have been in the milk was the never disputed fact that Thelma began to fall back to sleep or relapse back into a coma while she was being given the milk (according to Graham) or immediately afterwards (according to Stark). O'Leary asked Dr Gilmour:

> [t]he evidence was that she went back into the coma within five minutes of the administration of the milk? – Yes. Q. If that coma was induced by a . . . dose of veronal that dose must have been administered by an earlier dose of veronal? – All I can say is . . . [ellipses *not* ours!] Q. It couldn't have been administered in the milk – if those facts are correct? – *If it is correct that she was slipping into a coma at the time the milk was administered then in that case the veronal could not have been in the milk* [our emphasis].[36]

Although Dr Gilmour would later qualify this testimony by saying that for a variety of reasons the veronal would have been 'absorbed with great rapidity', he did not confirm that its absorption must have been – as Stark's evidence suggests –

virtually instantaneous. Instead, he told the court that 'I think my point was that it must have been given within half an hour of her going to sleep'[37] – which means that it may have been taken *before* the milk.

The Alternative Case

Thelma was clearly in a poor physical and mental state in the months before her death. Several witnesses confirm that when the curtain went down at the interval of the final performance of a play in which she was performing she took a considerable time to get to her feet. According to Mrs Bransgrove, everyone assumed she had had an attack of appendicitis (of which she would frequently complain) and was a 'heroine' for going on with the show. Stark testified that Thelma 'practically collapsed when she got home',[38] either because of 'the influence of liquor' or of 'nerves'. A few weeks before her death, Dr Walton examined Thelma on two separate occasions and found that she had been vomiting every morning in a way consistent with alcoholism (but not pregnancy), and was in a 'condition of nervous exhaustion'. O'Leary asked him whether 'you would have been surprised if you had heard she had committed suicide?' and Dr Walton answered, 'No, I wouldn't.'[39] Several witnesses, including Stark, also stated that Thelma had a dread of pregnancy and on more than one occasion confessed that she would rather die than have a child. The Mareos all claimed that Thelma would frequently spend long periods of time in bed because of illness. Stark did testify that on these occasions she was quite capable of looking after herself. However, when O'Leary asked her to confirm that Thelma had not been 'confined to her bed for two or three weeks continuously' she could only reply, 'She was in bed so much I can't really say.'[40]

What was contested, however, was Thelma's alleged alcoholism. This was crucial not just because it might have accounted for Mareo's delay in calling a doctor but it may also have called into question her general mental condition and therefore propensity to suicide or carelessness with other drugs, as well as the credibility of Stark. Although the autopsy indicated that Thelma showed no signs of alcoholism, that does not exclude the possibility in someone only twenty-nine years old. A number of witnesses who knew Thelma rather more casually than the main protagonists – Mrs Evans and Miss Bransgrove from the theatre and the various other visitors to the house – all reported that they had never seen her drunk. With the possible exception of the last night of the play, in which she collapsed, Stark maintained that she had never seen Thelma 'under the influence of liquor'.[41] Interestingly a number of witnesses confirmed that when Thelma did drink alcohol she would hold her nose. Stark maintained that she did this because '[s]he didn't like the taste of it very much',[42] although later under cross-examination she admitted that Thelma nevertheless 'liked the effect [of alcohol] – Oh yes, it made her feel better'.[43] However, in his statement to the police on the Tuesday after Thelma's arrest Mareo claimed that he was 'used to seeing my wife in an unconscious condition through alcohol' and that since the play Thelma had consumed 'on average two bottles of sherry every day'.[44] Betty and Graham confirmed their father's testimony.

On balance it seems that the case for Thelma's alcoholism was much stronger than the case for her relative sobriety for four main reasons. Firstly, while Stark's repeated denials that Thelma drank excessively were clearly crucial, when Mareo had asked her in front of the police only a few hours after Thelma's death whether she knew that 'Thelma used to drink a lot', Stark had replied, 'Oh yes, I did, Mr Mareo.'[45] Secondly, not much weight can be given to the evidence of those witnesses who knew her only casually and said they had never seen her drunk because it was precisely from such people that a heavy drinker could be expected to conceal their drinking successfully. Thirdly, Dr Walton's evidence should have been given considerable weight because he was the only witness professionally qualified to comment on Thelma's alleged alcoholism and the only witness who could not have had any reason to lie. Indeed, by stressing the seriousness of her mental and physical condition, Dr Walton may even have laid himself open to the suspicion that his treatment of her had been less than adequate.

Finally, and most tellingly, there is the sheer detail of the evidence given by Betty and Graham. Betty could remember an occasion towards the end of January when Thelma had been in bed for three weeks because 'she had been drinking';[46] being told by Stark on another occasion that her father hadn't drunk before marrying Thelma; a Saturday evening when Thelma had asked her to purchase some brandy and she had gone next door to 'the Wakeham's' and then been prevented from purchasing the alcohol by Mareo; and another occasion before Christmas when she had twice tried to prevent Stark from giving Thelma a bottle of colourless alcohol, the second time hiding it behind the piano. As well as claiming that Thelma was drunk after the Dixieland party and during the bathroom incident, Graham claimed to remember an occasion on which Thelma had given £1 of grocery money to Stark to buy liquor and he had called his father at the St James to tell him about it. The even more detailed evidence given by Mareo to the police on several occasions corroborates Graham's and Betty's testimony. Obviously, while the jury could not have been expected to treat Mareo's own children as impartial witnesses, they would nevertheless have had to credit the 17-year-old son and 21-year-old daughter with a considerable capacity for deceit. Interestingly, the autopsy revealed that Thelma did not suffer appendicitis or any kind of disease that might be confused with appendicitis. The Attorney-General, Mason, would later suggest that she feigned appendicitis to cover up her drinking.

O'Leary, then, proposed that Thelma had taken the veronal herself, although not necessarily with suicidal intent. He put it to the jury that

> On Saturday morning she was out of bed obviously searching for something, and either then or in the two hours when she was alone [between about 11.30 a.m. and 1.00 p.m.] she got veronal and swallowed it, and that was the veronal from which she died.

Throughout the Saturday she had no food or drink and her digestion was practically at a standstill, and the veronal would take hours to dissolve. She was aroused on Saturday night. She did not admit [sic] that she roused of her own volition. She was given sal volatile, which would greatly hasten the solution of the veronal remaining in the stomach [since it contained alcohol]. Then, in spite of the efforts of Miss Stark to keep her awake, she lapsed into unconsciousness and died. Death was due to the veronal taken on the Saturday morning, and it was not necessary for her to have taken it on Saturday night. [47]

There were several problems with this alternative account. No veronal was found in the bedroom, although of course that may have been because Thelma had consumed it. Alternatively, it may have been difficult for someone in her apparent condition to have gone to the laundry and reached up to the shelf where it was hidden, even though O'Leary told the jury that 'Poor little Detective Meiklejohn [who testified that he was "6'1/2" in [his] stocking"!] even had to get a chair to get up this shelf 5ft 7in. high! It was quite clear that Mrs Mareo could easily have got to the shelf.'[48] Finally, because of his decision to call no witnesses, O'Leary had no medical testimony to verify that the veronal would have remained reasonably inactive in her stomach until being dissolved by the sal volatile.

Nevertheless, all three doctors called by the Prosecution testified that Thelma must have had a dose of veronal on the Saturday morning. Dr Gilmour maintained that when Graham found Thelma swaying, incoherent and apparently looking for something, earlier on the Saturday morning, she may have been 'recovering from a dose taken on Friday night', or she may have been showing the 'preliminary symptoms from a dose taken on the Saturday morning. If they [re]present recovery from a dose on Friday night, then it is necessary to assume another dose on the Sat. morning'.[49] Dr Ludbrook thought it 'possible' that these symptoms may have 'immediately' followed the taking of a toxic dose, while Dr Gunson testified that Thelma took a dose of veronal on the Saturday morning, although he did not specify if this was when she was found by Graham swaying or somewhat later when Mareo was awake.[50] Not only did the three Crown doctors think that Thelma must have received a dose of veronal on the Saturday morning, but that this dose may have been taken just before or just after Graham found her swaying in front of the dresser. Since Mareo was not in the room at the time, according to the undisputed evidence of Graham, all three doctors had effectively testified that Thelma *may* have taken a dose of veronal by her own volition.

Thus the Crown had the seemingly impossible task of convincing the jury that Mareo had killed his wife with veronal when the evidence was entirely circumstantial and based on rather dubious medical testimony, when the dead person seems to have been quite capable of either endangering or taking her own life, and when by the Crown's own admission the deceased may have voluntarily taken somewhat earlier the same drug that later killed her. O'Leary's alternative account of the events had some problems but these paled into insignificance beside those of the Crown's. Moreover, the onus was on the Crown to convince the jury that its version of events was certain 'beyond reasonable doubt'.

It is of course easy for us more than half a century later to reconstruct painstakingly the complicated sequence of events. The jury could only be expected to take at most a few days to come to their decision. In recent years it has become clear that juries are usually confused after a long trial in which there is difficult and complex evidence. For example, one expert has found both that fewer than forty per cent of jurors in trials lasting two to three weeks claimed to have understood all of the trial and that there is a clear correlation between the length of the trial and the capacity of jurors to maintain concentration.[51] However, if the jury was confused then it had no alternative but to acquit Mareo, even if it had serious doubts about his innocence. Although the jury did apparently have some doubts, it seems that they were only about whether or not Mareo had intended to kill Thelma. A little over an hour after having retired to consider their verdict, the Foreman came back into the jury room and asked the judge whether or not there was a possibility of a manslaughter verdict. Mr Justice Arthur Fair, who would become known for the firmness with which he held his views and for the importance he attached to the dignity of his court, was conducting his first criminal trial as a judge. Perhaps for that reason his direction to the Foreman was ponderous and confusing, and completely failed to define what manslaughter was. Several hours later the Foreman came back into the court with the verdict 'Guilty, but with a strong recommendation for mercy'. Had the Foreman – who was a known opponent of capital punishment – convinced the others to recommend mercy? Or did the jury feel that in the light of the medical evidence they had no alternative but to deliver a guilty verdict about which they were nevertheless apprehensive? We can never know. Justice Fair, however, had no alternative by law but to don his black cap and sentence Mareo to be hanged.

CHAPTER THREE

The Second Trial

*'Say, listen Hazel,' Mrs Miller said, impressively, 'I'm telling
you I'd be awake for a year if I didn't take veronal. That stuff
makes you sleep like a fool.'*
'Isn't it poison, or something?' Mrs Morse asked.
*'Oh, you take too much and you're out for the count,' said
Mrs Miller. 'I just take five grains – they come in tablets. I'd be
scared to fool around with it. But five grains, and you cork off
pretty.'*
*'Can you get it anywhere?' Mrs Morse felt superbly
Machiavellian.*
*'Get all you want in Jersey,' said Mrs Miller. 'They won't
give it to you here without you have a doctor's prescription.'*
—Dorothy Parker, 'Big Blonde' (1929)

WHILE IN COURT on the second day of the trial, O'Leary
received a telegram from a man called Alex Whitington
living in Australia, stating: 'IF CALLED COULD GIVE MATERIAL
EVIDENCE SUPPORT DEFENCE MAREO CASE WRITING
TODAY.'[1] O'Leary cabled back 'WHAT IS NATURE OF
EVIDENCE' and Whitington responded the next day: 'HAVE
FREQUENTLY SEEN DECEASED BEFORE MARRIAGE
DEPRESSED TAKING VERONAL.'[2] In a letter to the Attorney-
General a little more than two weeks later, O'Leary explained
that '[a]fter receipt of this cablegram I communicated the
contents to the Crown Counsel but they stated, no doubt rightly,
that they could do nothing in the matter and I was left to take
what steps I felt disposed'.[3] Given the time it would have taken
to secure Whitington's presence in Auckland (he lived in Adelaide
which was about ten days away by ship), O'Leary had little
choice but to continue with the trial in the hope that his defence
of Mareo would be successful without Whitington's testimony,
and presumably knowing that, if it were not, he would be able

to seek a new trial on the basis of the new evidence which had come to light. Nevertheless, it must have been, to say the least, frustrating for O'Leary to know that there was now reasonably compelling and independent support for the misadventure/suicide theory, that could not be revealed to the Court.

As soon as the first trial was over and Mareo had been sentenced to death, O'Leary made an application to the trial judge for leave to appeal to the Court of Appeal on the grounds that the jury's verdict was against the weight of evidence. Before Mr Justice Fair could hear the application, O'Leary received a letter from Whitington, which elaborated upon the matters raised in his telegram. At that point it seems that O'Leary decided to make a further application for a retrial, this time under a statutory provision that allowed the Governor in Council to direct a new trial where he 'entertains a doubt whether such person ought to have been convicted'. O'Leary stated in his application to Mason that if this 'letter is genuine and I can see no reason for thinking otherwise, then Mr Whitington's information is of immense importance and as I have said above goes a long way in establishing the innocence of the accused'.[4] A short time later O'Leary received a letter dated 3 March from a Mrs Irene Riano of Melbourne, claiming amongst other things that she had known that Thelma had been 'addicted to headache powders and sleeping potions'.[5]

Prior to formulating advice to the Governor-General on the retrial application, Mason arranged for both Whitington and Riano to be interviewed by the Australian police. The Australian police also questioned a number of other people and took detailed statements from three of them: William Dawson, who had known the Mareos in Auckland and who confirmed that Thelma was a heavy drinker, 'appeared on the happiest of terms' with Mareo, and had said on one occasion, 'I would rather commit suicide than have an operation or a baby';[6] Hilda Hooper, a theatrical who had toured with Thelma, who stated that she had never seen her take 'any tablets other than aspros' or 'drink intoxicating liquor to excess' but who nevertheless believed '[s]he was of a very highly strung nature ... occasionally had an attack of appendix and used to express a horror of having an operation'[7]; and Herbert Kingsland, Mareo's 'right-hand man' for a time in Auckland, who said that the Mareos 'lived very happily together', and that Thelma was 'a heavy wine drinker', would 'frequently . . . take abnormal numbers of aspros out of a bottle, practically emptying the bottle' and 'was frequently sick for two or three days at a time and . . . [said] on several occasions that she would sooner commit suicide than have an operation or a child' and 'that she was having trouble with her appendix'.[8] Ultimately, Dawson was excused from giving evidence at the second trial because of work commitments and Hooper and Kingsland were not asked.

In the meantime, Mr Justice Fair had turned down the application for leave to appeal. No doubt eager to cover his bets, O'Leary appealed that decision and was heard by a full bench (five judges) of the Court of Appeal between 23 and 26 March 1936. He must have known, however, that it would be an uphill battle. Only in exceptional cases will an appellate court (whose members have not had the benefit of seeing the witnesses or hearing their testimony) declare itself willing to 'second-guess' a jury on matters relating to witness credibility and the determination of issues of fact. Nevertheless, O'Leary valiantly argued that, in failing properly to discount or exclude the possibility that Thelma had administered the veronal to herself, the Prosecution had not proved its case beyond reasonable doubt and the verdict was therefore 'against the weight of evidence'. On 8 April, the Court of Appeal delivered two judgements that unanimously rejected O'Leary's arguments, finding that the jury was entitled to interpret the evidence as it (manifestly) had, and that while the alternative theory put forward by the Defence (that Thelma had caused her own death) was tenable, the jury's rejection of it was not beyond the pale.

Nevertheless, O'Leary's alternative application was granted and on 22 April 1936 the Prime Minister advised the Governor-General to order a new trial, which he duly did. Three days later, O'Leary's instructing solicitor, Mr K.C. Aekins, made a further application to have the second trial held in Wellington on the grounds that, because of Mareo's 'prominent position', the public prejudice against him, and the 'more than ordinary interest' 'excited' by his case, he 'would not receive an impartial trial in that city'.[9] Mason replied by cable: 'I HAVE HAD ENQUIRIES MADE AND GIVEN CAREFUL CONSIDERATION AND NETT RESULT IN MY OPINION DOES NOT DISCLOSE SUFFICIENT GROUND TO WARRANT CHANGE OF VENUE.'[10] The second trial took place in Auckland and lasted from 1–17 June, a comparatively long time then for a criminal trial. Apart from its length, it differed from the first in four main ways: there was a new Crown Prosecutor, new evidence for the Defence, more contradictory evidence from the Crown's medical witnesses, and a new trial judge, the staunch Roman Catholic, Mr Justice Callan. Except for the first, all of these differences were or should have been substantially in Mareo's favour.

The New Crown Prosecutor

The new senior counsel for the Crown was (later Sir) Vincent Meredith. Meredith called only three new witnesses, two of whom took the stand for very brief periods and had nothing to add to the evidence of other witnesses, and a third witness, a former theatrical from Adelaide who had worked with Thelma, and who testified that in the five or six weeks he had known her he had never seen her taking veronal or 'dopey and depressed'.[10] As for the substance of his case, it was much the same as his predecessor's, except for an extremely ingenious explanation of Mareo's apparently guilty behaviour about Morgan's drugs and lack of guilt about the veronal. In his summing-up, Meredith's predecessor had not dealt with this issue at all. By contrast, Meredith argued that Mareo had repeatedly lied about Morgan's drugs so that it would appear that he had a bad conscience about an abortifacient. In other words, Mareo *feigned* deceit about Morgan's drugs in order to provide a smoke-screen for his real guilt about the veronal. But why would Mareo have devised such a risky plan? After all, the penalty for procuring and administering abortifacients at the time was life imprisonment. And why would someone so fiendishly clever as to lay such a false trail jeopardise its efficacy with a story about his wife's lesbianism? Why would a man who wanted people to believe that he had guiltily purchased an abortifacient for his wife at the same time allege that she had no interest in sexual intercourse with men?

Nevertheless, it seems Meredith was able to camouflage such bizarre logic with his courtroom presence and rhetoric. A politically conservative man who regularly appealed the 'very pro-Maori' rulings of Judge Acheson (the author of the novel Mareo was adapting for screen), Meredith was at the time the manager of the All Blacks and a 'star' performer on the amateur stage as well as in court. But for his sporting commitments overseas, Meredith would have conducted the first trial as well. Of this distinguished performer it has been said that

> [W]ith an abundance of forensic talent, with a glorious control of voice and yet with a common touch which enabled him to communicate his point of view in the simple language of which he was the master, he was indeed a formidable figure. The lesson which he could teach above all others was that of simplicity. His guiding principle was that if a law could not be explained and comprehended as sensible and right by an ordinary layman, it could not and should not be enforced. It was his facility and understanding of the mind of the witness and of the point of view of the jury which enabled him to be more effective than many who may have been his legalistic masters. [11]

In addition to his undoubted advocacy skills, it seems that Meredith brought with him to the second trial a determination to secure a conviction that probably exceeded a prosecutor's usual drive to win. The extent of the competition he felt with his predecessor, Alexander Johnstone KC, ought not be underestimated. It would not have looked well for the Auckland Crown Solicitor (who had successfully prosecuted two recent and prominent poisoning cases) to achieve an inferior result to Johnstone, who had effectively been only a last-minute ring in.

Thus Meredith's questioning of the Defence's witnesses was at times aggressive, and he also emphasised to a far greater degree than his predecessor the vile nature of Mareo's accusations against his wife. For example, while in the first trial Johnstone alleged that Mareo had 'blackened' his wife's name with the lesbian accusation, Meredith added the melodramatic embellishment that this was only done when 'Mrs Mareo's tongue is now stilled'. Whether as a result Meredith indeed indulged in 'overkill' was a question that was to trouble the Attorney-General in his review of the case in subsequent years. Certainly he was an interesting contrast to O'Leary with all his shyness towards women. Meredith was the right man to make a lesbian charge rebound on the accuser, O'Leary the wrong man to make it stick.

New Evidence for the Defence

Whitington testified that he had read about the Mareo trial in an Adelaide newspaper and had decided to contact O'Leary because he had seen Thelma taking veronal on 'at least a dozen occasions' and had also observed that she was frequently 'very depressed'.[12] At the start of his testimony he told the court that he had seen Mareo 'for the first time just now'.[13] However, while Whitington took pains to describe Thelma as a 'particularly straight virtuous girl', he may not have appeared to the jury as a particularly virtuous man. After all, the young accountant had frequently visited the single actress in her various hotel and bedsitting rooms, some of which were far from his home town of Adelaide. He had first seen Thelma perform in Adelaide towards the end of 1928, then early the next year at Port Pirie, a town 140 miles north of Adelaide, and at Kapunda or the Burra, even more remote towns, then in Adelaide again in 1930 and 1931, and finally in Melbourne while he was on holiday towards the end of 1931. Either some of these meetings must have been remarkable coincidences, or Whitington was taking great pains in pursuing the actress over such long distances.

When asked by Meredith why he chose to spend so much time with someone he had described as 'not a cheerful companion', Whitington replied:

> I was interested in her case and I rather admired her in lots of ways. I was married at the time. Mrs Whitington was not interested in her case. I was separated from my wife at the time, prior to knowing Miss Trott, and all the time I did know her.[14]

Perhaps the jury believed that Whitington was a spurned suitor acting out of spite. Nevertheless, to make such a journey both in aid of a man he had never met and in order to blacken the name of a dead woman who had rejected his romantic advances seems highly unlikely.

Similarly, while the testimony of the Defence's other Australian witnesses was also unambiguous, they may have struck the jury as not particularly reliable. Like Whitington, Mrs Irene Riano had read about the trial in the newspaper and decided to contact the relevant authorities because she had frequently seen Thelma taking veronal and threatening suicide. The last of these occasions was when the manager of the Ernest C. Rolls Revue Company, for which Thelma worked, had told her she would not be touring New Zealand. According to Mrs Riano, 'Miss Trott so convinced them that she would do away with herself unless they took her that they decided to take her over to New Zealand.'[15] Yet, while Mrs Riano was not herself a practising 'theatrical' and therefore untainted by the nonconformity of that profession, she did accompany her daughter and granddaughter, who were both actresses, on tour. Mrs Riano was a widow and neither her daughter nor granddaughter was accompanied by husbands. Her granddaughter, Miss Jane Riano Neil, also testified at the trial, confirming her grandmother's statements about Thelma's drinking habits and depressive behaviour, but adding that on the voyage to Auckland she had seen on 'a ledge alongside Thelma's bunk . . . a bottle . . . [with] the word Barbitone [another name for veronal] on it.'[16] Jane usually used her mother's maiden name, Riano, and was an

American citizen, having been born in that country. Although Meredith did not question the Rianos about their unusually constituted family, he did imply that their testimony was not entirely impartial. Jane Riano confessed that Thelma 'picked me up a little sharp' and had 'told me once to mind my own business' when 'she was under the influence of liquor', but she did maintain that she 'liked Miss Trott'. Meredith mysteriously inquired whether her 'mother asked Miss Trott to find out where a certain man in the show was spending his time and Miss Trott said she would not do that sort of thing for any man', but Jane Riano denied this and claimed that her 'mother was very fond of Thelma'.[17] However, despite such cross-examination, there was very little Meredith could do about the fact that Irene Riano had written an entirely unsolicited letter to O'Leary informing him of Thelma's 'excessive use of drugs'. Perhaps the Rianos did strike the men of the jury as an unconventional family, but, again, a long trip across the Tasman in order to tell lies about the drug addiction of a dead woman and thereby defend a man whom they had known for only a few weeks should also have seemed most improbable.

O'Leary also called a number of other witnesses to support his theory that Thelma died from a self-administered dose of veronal taken on the Saturday morning, the most important of whom was a former examiner in Toxicology and Medical Jurisprudence at the University of New Zealand, Dr E.W. Giesen. The three main aspects of Dr Giesen's testimony were that: (1) the Crown's medical experts interpreted both the available medical literature and Thelma's symptoms incorrectly; (2) because she had had nothing to eat or drink since the Friday night, veronal would have remained undigested in her stomach during the Saturday until it was acted on that evening by the water, sal volatile and milk; and (3) when on the Saturday morning Graham found Thelma disoriented and apparently looking for something in a half-open drawer, she was suffering from what was called 'automatism', a condition in which a patient already under the influence of a drug unconsciously seeks and then takes further unnecessary doses. As for the theory of 'automatism',

O'Leary also called in support of Dr Giesen the wife of an orchardist, who remembered searching for some veronal and taking it while strongly under the influence of a previous dose, and a schoolmaster, who testified that on one occasion he had passed out in his bathroom, woken, and 'concluded . . . [that he] was looking for Veronal'.[18]

In fact, we now know that, like all barbiturates, veronal can indeed present a real danger of 'automatism' (from which, according to one theory, Marilyn Monroe was suffering when she died). Furthermore, a person can build up a tolerance for barbiturates such as veronal, at which point the higher dose required to produce the same effect is not much less than a fatal dose. However, even at the time the so-called 'hypnotic' effects of veronal were well documented.[19]

The Crown's Medical Witnesses

It is of course very difficult to determine the kind of impression the Crown's medical witnesses made in the courtroom. Nevertheless, the transcript of the second trial does indicate that the *substance* of their testimony was often extremely unconvincing. For example, at one stage under cross-examination, Dr Gilmour admitted that 'there is no evidence that she was in a coma throughout Saturday, at any stage of the day at all', then almost immediately contradicted himself by reiterating the general proposition that a persona cannot 'relapse' 'from *coma* back into coma' [our emphasis] without another dose of veronal. When alerted by O'Leary to this contradiction, he maintained that his proposition was that a person will recover from merely an 'overdose', even though this weakened the principle or theory by making it extend to rather minor cases of poisoning.[20] At one point Dr Gunson agreed with O'Leary that his 'opinions' were 'sweeping', and then went on to make the astounding admission that these opinions were 'impossible to check'.[21] And Dr Ludbrook told the court that if the 'theory' about the impossibility of relapsing into a coma

A. . . . is wrong, it is no use to prove a murder.

Q. If it is shown that there are exceptions to it, I suggest to you it is no use to prove a murder.

A. Not necessarily, because I do not think you can get two cases in which all the circumstance are exactly the same.

Q. Then what is the good of the theory?

A. It is not a theory, it is an opinion based on evidence placed before us. [22]

Of course such imprecision is only to be expected during oral testimony given under considerable pressure. However, on at least one occasion Dr Gilmour was simply wrong. For example, he told the court 'that in taking the quantities recovered from the organs, one takes into consonance the fact that veronal is more or less equally distributed throughout the body'. [23] According to the relevant medical authority, Witthaus's *Manual of Toxicology*, however, 'the distribution in the different organs and tissues is uneven under all circumstances, and the quantity in one part is no indication of that in any other'. [24] Not only had the Defence's medical witness gone to some trouble to explain Dr Gilmour's basic error, but the judge had even read the relevant passage out in court.

Mr Justice Callan's Summing Up

Although it was not in Justice Callan's power to direct the jury to acquit Mareo, it is clear that he believed that most of the links in the Crown's long chain of reasoning were extremely weak. He pointed out that the supposed proposition of Sir William Willcox's about veronal – on which the Prosecution's case almost entirely depended – was not 'universally accepted'. [25] However, even if it had been accepted as medical fact – and the judge pointed out that the Crown required nothing less than that – then it did 'not fit this case as described by the Crown witnesses', since the proposition applied only to patients initially in a coma. Although Dr Giesen was wrong to maintain that there 'were no gastric juices in a fasting stomach', since no one had thought to ask any of the doctors whether the rate of absorption might be considerably slower, Dr Giesen's theory was very far from disproved.[26] He questioned whether Dr Gilmour – who maintained that he had changed his mind after hearing Stark's final cross-examination at the first trial – 'could ... be relied upon' when he 'shrank from saying the fatal quantity could have been in one portion of the cup and yet . . . [was] satisfied that it could have been in this other not much larger quantity of milk?'[27] As for the non-medical aspects of the case, Justice Callan said that Whitington's 'actions [in volunteering to testify] . . . speak honesty'.[28] He pointed out that a man who kills himself as well as his wife would not also 'enjoy the society of Eleanor Brownlee'.[29] And he thought that if Mareo had been lying about Morgan's drugs then this 'would bespeak a very considerable degree of foresight',[30] but that if Mareo's guilt about Morgan's drugs had been real rather than feigned then this might explain 'a tremendous number of facts which look very black against him particularly his obvious reluctance and failure to send for a doctor'.[31] Finally, he raised very cautiously the possibility of a manslaughter verdict, asking the jury to consider carefully whether 'there [was] anything to suggest that his mind was not working sufficiently well for him to know what he was doing'.[32]

Verdict and Judgement

The jury retired for only two-and-a-half hours, during which time they took dinner. At the first trial the jury had deliberated for three times as long even though the trial was half the length. Like the first jury, this second jury returned the verdict of guilty of murder, except that this time there was no recommendation for mercy.

The scene in court when the verdict was announced was dramatic. The *Auckland Star* reported that Mareo 'stepped back a pace as though stunned. Then he turned to the girl, murmuring, "Betty . . . Betty . . ."'[33] The registrar then asked if the prisoner had 'anything to say why the sentence of death should not be passed', and Mareo replied

> [I]t is very hard to say anything under the circumstances, because it is the second time I have been through this terrible ordeal. I can only say that it seems to me, from a logical, clear-minded man's reasoning, from the way the whole of this case has been conducted by all the counsel, and after your Honor's, may I say, marvelous summing-up, I have been sentenced on the lying word of Freda Stark. I ought not to say that, but what can I say? Nothing more.[34]

After the judgement of death had been pronounced, the *Star* observed that

> [B]ending low over the table, his head in his hands, sobbing audibly sat Mr Humphrey O'Leary, a tired, disillusioned man. Behind him sat Betty Mareo, trying hard to choke back the tears. A woman consoled her.[35]

One commentator was to say some thirty years later (and sixteen years after his death) that O'Leary's 'greatest disappointment was, I think, his failure in 1936 to secure the acquittal of Mareo on his second trial for the murder of his wife by veronal poisoning'.[36] As for the prisoner, the *Star* also reported that

> [A] warder touched Mareo on the shoulder, an indication that he was to go back to prison – back to he knew not what. With tragic appeal his lips twice formed the word 'Betty' as he looked across at the girl who had know him as her father. She tried to smile through a flood of tears. Mareo turned, and as though in a daze, moved towards the dock staircase which leads to the cells. He had walked down three, when he turned and tried to go back.
>
> A warder quietly urged him down. 'I want to see Betty,' he said. Then he disappeared.[37]

CHAPTER FOUR

Who Was Eric Mareo?

She accompanied him to the orchestra entrance where, in a few minutes' time, they were joined by Leila Garland and Luis da Soto – the perfect platinum blonde and the perfect lounge-lizard. . . . As for da Soto, he looked harmless enough, and did not seem to have any pressing reason for doing away with Alexis. One never knew, of course, with these slinky people of confused nationality.
—Dorothy L. Sayers, *Have His Carcase* (1932)

ALTHOUGH MAREO WAS something of a minor celebrity before his arrest, many Aucklanders would have distrusted him. The size and isolation of New Zealand no doubt generated enthusiasm for visiting 'theatricals', but it also would have fuelled suspicion. Two days before the opening of the first trial, the *Herald* observed in a context unrelated to Mareo that, while '[t]he idea that all musicians, artists, and actors are temperamental, inconsistent, eccentric in their private lives' was a 'fallacy', it had 'increased rather than diminished during the last few years', at least according to the wife of a 'popular English dance band leader'.[1] In the same year the *Weekly News* could proudly remark '[t]hat what may be roughly indicated as the jazz elements in social life have hardly touched New Zealand', and that as a consequence most New Zealanders were content to dine early and at home, their once-in-a-lifetime reward of 'seeing Europe' meaning 'Great Britain with a few contiguous foreign places of interest'.[2] No doubt it was largely from such 'foreign places' that musicians and actors came. For, as the *Herald*'s music and drama critic complained in the year of Mareo's arrest,

[w]hen the child of uncompromisingly British parents shows an instinctive desire for music his father frequently does his

best to eliminate it. Music, to the British mind, is always suspect. It is manly enough and respectable enough to be a merchant, or a lawyer, or a grocer, but there is some taint of femininity about the arts – something wild and long-haired and unbusiness-like. Many a young man has been forced by a fat-headed father to drop the musical career which would have kept him interested and happy, either for this reason or because there is 'no money in it'.[3]

Accordingly, the Wellington Symphony Orchestra was conducted by Leon de Mauny, the Dunedin Philharmonic by Signor Squarise and the two Christchurch orchestras in the first three decades of the century by Benno Scherek, Alfred Bünz and Angus Gunter (as well as Alfred Worsley).[4]

Mareo seems to have fitted the foreign stereotype perfectly. After the trials *Truth* remembered that he would walk up and down the main street of Auckland 'cheerily greet[ing] his acquaintances with "Hello, hello"'.[5] On such occasions, according to the *Observer*, he would often be seen with

a cigarette holder in one hand, a cane and gloves in the other. That long white cigarette holder was by itself sufficient to attract attention to the man. He used to walk down Queen Street with one end of it in his mouth, the other sticking out rakishly about a foot in front of him.

It was typical of Mareo that, when the success of his symphony concerts made him a well-known figure in the city, he persuaded a well-known Queen Street tobacconist to place in his window a large photograph of himself, with cigarette holder. Underneath ran the legend: 'We stock the Mareo cigarette holder.'[6]

There were many such stories told about Mareo. For example, one newspaper reported that

during lunch in a North Island country hotel the other day, a correspondent has written to 'Truth', the inevitable subject of Mareo arose. A young traveller joined in the conversation, saying he spent three months in the same boardinghouse as the

Mareos in Auckland. That was in the days before they went to the Tenterden Avenue house that was to be the last home for the actress-wife.

The traveller said the boarders noticed one peculiarity in particular in Mareo, who, it was said, would rise in the morning and attire himself in a dress suit, even to the white bowtie.

He would go out on the front lawn and walk up and down, smoking a cigarette in an exceptionally long holder. The cigarette completed, Mareo would return to his room, remove the dress suit, and have his shave and bath.[7]

Although no doubt initially an affectation, the cigarette holder seems to have become a habit with Mareo. According to the ambulance driver who took Thelma to the hospital (but who was not called at the trials), Mareo was 'smoking a cigarette in a long holder' when he arrived at Tenterden Avenue.[8]

Such theatricality carried over into his concerts. The *Observer* reported that '[t]ouches of showmanship contributed to the popular success' of the Mareo Symphony Orchestra's concerts:

[T]he stage was decked in crimson roses. Every music stand trailed its garland. Busts of great composers stood in the background and the name 'Mareo' was outlined in flowers. For the first time, a battery of bright lights was hung low over the orchestras, as at a wrestling match, while the rest of the hall was darkened. When Mareo entered, the players rose and clapped him. Some of them felt rather self-conscious about this, but Mareo had explained beforehand that he expected it not as a personal tribute but as part of the general scheme of showmanship which he considered indispensable in 'putting it over'.

There was also the tinseled baton. Some musicians considered this to be in bad taste, but one man who worked with Mareo said the primary purpose of the tinsel was to make the baton glitter so that the players, not the public could see it.[9]

Needless to say, such a performer would have been distrusted in a country whose 'climate of opinion' at the time has been characterised by P.J. Gibbons as one in which there was on the one hand the existence of a tiny minority who held values opposed to those which generally prevailed, who were willing to express their opinions, and who had access to a forum in which they could be expressed; on the other hand the intolerance of dissent, even by a Labour Government whose members had once been feared as disloyal socialists, and the willingness of large number of New Zealanders to fight for race and empire.[10]

Moreover, a reckless spender like Mareo would have stood out in a climate of severe economic austerity. Although, like about 12–15 per cent of the New Zealand workforce, Mareo was out of work at the time of Thelma's death, there seems to have been little sympathy for his plight.[11] Indeed, his desperate financial condition was only ever referred to as implying weak moral fibre and, more ominously, as a reason for murder. This is hardly surprising, given that in virtually all other respects Mareo was quite unlike the unemployed. One man who lived through the Depression later remembered that

> [T]hings got very rundown . . . First of all the clothing was very bad and the old clothes drives started to disappear because there were no old clothes – people were wearing them. The obvious thing was, if you saw a photograph of a crowd, you could tell that those people were suffering.[12]

When the dapper Mareo walked down Queen Street – where just a year or two earlier the unemployed had rioted – his cigarette holder alone must have verged on a provocation for many.

Nevertheless, 'types' like Mareo were not entirely unfamiliar to Aucklanders. Although few New Zealand men were accustomed to wearing tuxedos in the morning, the social historian Danielle Sprecher has found that one department store during the early 1930s instructed its salesmen to recognise not just the careful and careless dresser but also what it called the 'sheik type' (albeit to 'give him all the rope he wants'!), a fact that rather 'throws doubt upon the ubiquity of the usual stereotype of the rugby-playing, hard-drinking bloke who did not care a toss about what he wore or what he bought'.[13] However, as the very term 'sheik' suggests, such flamboyant dressing, even when practised by a local, was associated with the 'foreign' or 'exotic'. Indeed, there can be no doubt that the use of the term here derived from two films, *The Sheik* (1921) and *The Son of a Sheik* (1926), both starring, significantly, that epitome of Italian charisma, Rudolph Valentino. Although Mareo did speak with a Received Pronunciation accent and the *Observer* described him before his arrest as a '[m]uch-travelled English-man',[14] his Italian-sounding name and his frequently observed habit of speaking in an 'excitable', 'emotional' and 'rapid' manner had him marked as a somewhat dubious 'Latin type'.

In fact, Mareo's actual nationality became a topic of much speculation, as one would expect in a country in which during the 1930s only about 0.3 per cent of the New Zealand population were from the other side of the English Channel (Australia had twice and Canada ten times that percentage[15]). After the first trial, *Truth* reported that

> [c]onsiderable curiosity has been aroused over Mareo's nationality . . . One man who has been in close touch with Mareo of late, when approached by 'Truth' to throw some light on it, replied that he knew, but that he would be committing a breach of trust if he divulged it.[16]

During both trials it was well known that he spoke fluent German, and after the first *Truth* divulged that it 'is informed elsewhere that Mareo's parents are Austrians, and his father and stepmother live in Sydney'.[17] In fact, a police report revealed that Mareo's original names were Eric Joachim Pechotsch and that he had been 'born in Sydney, Australia, on 30th September 1891 and attended school there. His father's name is Raimunda Pechotsch, a Professor of Music at Sydney.'[18] This became known shortly after his arrest. However, while not much else was publicly known, it is worth briefly describing Mareo's family since it allows us to understand what kind of person he was.

Mareo's father, Raimund Leo Pechotsch, had arrived in

Australia with a Viennese band and settled there with his two brothers, Rupert and Adolf. Raimund worked as the director of the St Stephen's Cathedral Choir in Brisbane. Some years later he returned to Europe where he was the Musical Director of the Lyceum Theatre Orchestra in London, and then a Principal Professor at the prestigious Guildhall School of Music, also in London. During this period the 13-year-old Eric began his musical studies in Berlin under the Polish composer and pianist Xavier Scharwenka, a man who is today largely forgotten but was, in his time, thought by some to be the equal of Liszt as a pianist, and his superior as a composer. Sometime before or just after the outbreak of war, Raimund returned to Australia where he worked as a private teacher of violin, singing and piano.

Mareo's elder brother, also named Raimund, was regarded as something of a child prodigy on the violin, and in 1897 performed at the Portman Rooms in London at the age of 14. After touring Australia with the American Concert singer, Belle Cole, he commenced a solo career, performing, composing and recording under the name of Jan Rudenyi (Mareo's penchant for pseudonyms was plainly a family trait). Later, however, Raimund junior was to abandon 'classical' music, joining the well-regarded Moss and Stoll Music Hall circuit, before his early death from complications of diabetes during the First World War.

Mareo's mother was born Elizabeth Mary Dolman and had recently been widowed when she married Raimund Pechotsch in 1880. By then, she already had two sons by her first husband, Peter Curtis, one of whom was later to become a well-known Australian King's Counsel and, presumably in his spare time, something of a librettist. Both Mareo's mother's maiden name and the name she took on her first marriage were later to provide the basis for two of Eric's *alter egos* – Eric Dolman and (on his release from jail) Eric Curtis.

In the course of their investigations in 1935, the New Zealand police identified a further five names by which Mareo was known in England: Edgar Martell, Guy Franklyn, Evan Marsden, Garry Foster and Leo Varney. Although it appears that these names were true noms de plume, in that Mareo used them professionally rather than privately, their very existence appears to have deepened police suspicions about him. And there were other aspects of Mareo's life that did nothing to allay the police concern that they were dealing with a shifty and possibly criminal character. In addition to the speculation about and inquiry into the question of his nationality, to which we have already referred, his place and date of birth also became the subject of close official scrutiny.

Although Mareo's own statement as to his birthdate accorded with the information recorded in his passport, and was confirmed by his father, the police sought confirmation from the Registrar General in Sydney but found that the birth was not registered there. When this was put to Mareo's father, Pechotsch said he must simply have overlooked the registration 'owing to the pressure of business in 1891'. Still not satisfied, the police searched the parish register of St Francis's Roman Catholic Church in Paddington. Here they found Eric's baptism recorded on 18 October 1891, and his given date of birth confirmed.[19]

The police also instigated thorough inquiries into the rumours that were rife in Auckland at the time of his arrest about the existence of a previous Mrs Mareo. According to the application to have the second trial held out of Auckland, one of these 'persistent rumour[s]' was that 'Mareo's previous wife had died in peculiar circumstances'.[20] Inquiries of New Scotland Yard and of the Registrar of Deaths in the United Kingdom revealed that the woman concerned had indisputably died of 'tuberculosis in England in 1928' and that Mareo had nursed her through the final stages of her illness.

However the reports received from Scotland Yard also revealed less salutary facts about Mareo's English life. The summary of them prepared by the key police witness at the trials, Detective Sergeant Arnold Bell Meiklejohn, recorded that

[a]bout 1913 when Dr. Herbert Edward Gray, late of Esher, Surrey, and his wife were staying at the seaside they met Mareo

who is believed to have been pianist in a pierrot show and Mrs. Gray ran away with him. When Gray heard of his wife's pregnancy he insisted that the child should be born in his house. He took her to Esher where Elizabeth Patricia was born. She went back to Mareo and about four years later Gray heard his wife was ill and found her living with Mareo in squalid surroundings, and again pregnant. Gray again insisted that the child [Graham] should be born in his house and after the birth Mrs. Gray went away to live with Mareo. Mareo and Mrs. Gray rejoiced in the fact that both children were theirs and taunted Gray with this. Gray never divorced his wife. Gray made generous allowances to Mareo for the education and clothing of the two children. Numerous payments were made by Gray through Mr. Carn, Solicitor, to Mareo, mainly by cheque. In March 1930 Mareo demanded from Gray £91 about this time for Mareo to settle some debts for board for the two children. Instead Mareo spent all this money in purchasing a motor boat. Mareo left for Sydney in December 1930 owing school and hotel fees for the two children. He wrote Gray threatening action if £80 was not paid at once. Gray instructed Carn to cease remittances and liquidate all debts. One of Mareo's debts in England when he left was to a Mr. Larway when he owed this man £600 up to 1930.

. . . Six years prior to this (1920) Mareo met a Miss Nora Bailey, a professional violinist and he lived with her and she was known as Mrs. Mareo. He was usually away at weekends and thus it will be seen that for six years he associated with the two women. Mrs. Mareo (Nora Bailey) did not hear from him after he left England in 1930. From 1927 to 1930 he was continually in the company of a Miss Sexton in England but she cannot be traced.[21]

Meiklejohn had also learned that Mareo's relocation to Australia in 1930 had not materially altered his pattern of behaviour. His report went on to reveal that:

[w]hile in Australia Mareo conducted orchestras in Sydney on his arrival there but for about eighteen months he was out of work. While there he became engaged to a Miss Stone, a professional dancer, and while still engaged to her married Thelma Trott on 18th October 1933. During the engagement

he borrowed about £300 from the mother of Miss Stone. This woman says she practically kept Mareo and the two children for the eighteen months he was out of work. He contracted debts in Sydney and was also known as a heavy drinker. He was heavily in debt in Auckland and a persistent drinker.

A leading orchestra leader in Sydney told Mrs. Stone that Mareo was known to them as 'The Gentleman Crook'.

Miss Stone on being informed that Mareo had married in New Zealand became hysterical.

When the Stones' allegations were put to Mareo by the police after his arrest, his rather typical response was that they 'are crook spiritualists . . . [who] tried to blackmail me when I came to N.Z. but I sent a stinging letter in reply threatening police action and never heard any more'.[22]

In fact, the Stones were expatriate New Zealanders who clearly retained some affection for Mareo notwithstanding his rather shabby treatment of them. The statements they made to the New Zealand police in June 1935 are hardly vitriolic, with Mrs Stone saying: 'I knew from my observations that Mareo used to drink, but otherwise his conduct was well-behaved, and was all I could have desired for my daughter.' Similarly, Irene Stone rather wistfully told the police that '[f]or all the time that I was with him he was everything that I could wish for . . .'[23] Interestingly, the Stones' capacity for a degree of forgiveness seems to have been shared by most if not all who were taken in by Mareo. Even in a time of economic depression, none of the many people who were owed money by him seemed particularly to begrudge the loans they had made, and, as we shall see, the devotion of Nora Bailey, who had been so cruelly abandoned by Mareo in 1930, was to last for nearly three decades.

As far as the Stones were concerned, it seems Mareo eventually did the honourable thing and requested the police to return those items of their property he had in his possession. In a mildly diverting epilogue to their involvement in our story, it seems that in Wellington in January 1936, Irene Stone married Barton Albert Ginger of Hataitai who had starred in the 1927

New Zealand film *Under the Southern Cross*. Somewhat ironically, Ginger's character in the film, Robert Fenton, was an English fraudster who has 'framed' the hero for crimes he had himself committed in the 'old country'. However, after trying to marry the local heroine for her money, Fenton gets his just deserts and the hero gets the girl.

Nor does it seem that Mareo left his old habits behind when he came to Auckland and married Thelma. Melville Harcourt, a clergyman who wrote a book soon after the trials in support of Mareo called *I Appeal*, claimed that

> Mareo's undeniable attraction for many women, his apparent willingness to philander when opportunity occurred, [and] his weakness for attitudinising didn't . . . commend him to the men of the community. The silver baton, the supercilious tilt of the head, the impeccable dress-clothes 'needled' the men. Perhaps they were a little envious, as much as it attracted their wives and sweethearts who were charmed by the music of this gaily-plumed bird that had alighted so unexpectedly in their midst. Mareo, unwisely maybe, was completely indifferent to the resentment of the men, and frankly flattered by the admiration of the women.[24]

Whether or not Mareo had affairs with other women in New Zealand we do not know. He may well have had the inclination, but not the ability to follow it through. His junior counsel at the time, Trevor Henry, told us that Mareo claimed that veronal had made him impotent.

Thus after his arrest it is not surprising that people believed him to be a bounder and a cad. His personality and his willingness to rack up large debts in pursuit of a glamorous lifestyle would have rankled some and produced resentment at a time when many were responding more frugally to economic hardship. His profession and nationality were, respectively, dubious and uncertain. But, above all, his marriage to a woman who had some money, and the ease with which he spent it, would have seemed consistent with what was known about his previous relationships with women.

Nevertheless, the kind of hostility that Mareo may have provoked was hardly sufficient to overcome the flaws in the Crown's case. One doesn't send a man to the gallows on the basis of that kind of evidence. And of course the dead woman and the Crown's principal witness were also theatricals about whom tales had been told. If the jury were all too ready to believe the worst of Mareo, it seems they were equally ready to give Thelma and Stark the benefit of the doubt. How was it that Mareo's lesbian accusation could be disbelieved and consequently held against him?

CHAPTER FIVE

The Lesbian Accusation

*If Christianity does not destroy this doctrine [of homosexuality],
then this doctrine will destroy it, together with the civilisation
it has built on the ruins of paganism. . . . I would rather give a
healthy boy or a healthy girl a phial of prussic acid than this
novel. Poison kills the body, but moral poison kills the soul.*
—James Douglas, editor of the London *Sunday Express*,
on Radclyffe Hall's *The Well of Loneliness* (1928)

WE CAN NOW BE reasonably sure that Mareo was not lying about his wife's sexual preferences. For at least the last two decades of the last century Stark was 'out' as a lesbian, during which time she frequently stated or implied that she and Thelma were more than 'bosom friends'. It is possible, of course, that the Mareos did have sexual intercourse. Nomenclature was rather uncertain at the time and perhaps by 'lesbian' Mareo meant 'bisexual'. However, it is more likely that their marriage was principally one of convenience and that Mareo was telling the police the truth when he said that they had 'agreed before we were married that we would not have sexual intercourse and I have not broken that promise'.[1] Mareo was newly arrived in the country, in debt and in need of money for his various theatrical projects. In addition to her vulnerable psychological condition, Thelma's professional life was inherently precarious. Thus, with his musical talent and entrepreneurial energy, Mareo would have promised some degree of job security. Besides, as many witnesses and even Stark on one occasion testified, it is also quite likely that they did get on reasonably well together. Marriages of convenience were, of course, not uncommon; in later years Stark would herself marry the homosexual dancer Harold Robinson.

Despite the evidence to the contrary, it seems most unlikely that the juries and the wider public (as opposed to their close circle of friends) believed that Thelma and Stark were 'lesbians'.

How could the juries have found Mareo guilty if they had believed that his wife was a 'lesbian' and therefore according to prevailing 'wisdom' a person with every reason to kill herself? How could the juries have believed the Crown's very speculative and shaky medical case if, by the admission of its own medical experts, it rested almost entirely on the testimony of someone who enjoyed, in the words of Mr Justice Fair, 'sexual perversion' of 'such a gross nature'?[2] And surely, if the all-male juries had believed that Stark and Thelma were 'lesbians', they would have felt enough sympathy for the accused to have found some 'reasonable doubt' in the Crown's case. Significantly, it was never suggested at the time in court, the newspapers or, to the best of our knowledge, anywhere else, that Mareo might have killed his wife because he was furious or jealous that she was having an affair with a woman. Clearly, while Thelma and Stark's close circle of friends might have believed that they were lovers, virtually no one else did.[3] Thus, since the Crown made so much of his attempt to 'blacken' his wife's name, it seems that his 'accusation' did reflect very badly on his character. If we can explain why the juries did not believe Mareo then perhaps we can in part account for why they believed he was guilty.

Part of the reason that Mareo's 'accusation' did not stick was that his counsel, O'Leary, was reluctant to make it do so. O'Leary never asked Stark directly whether she had been having a sexual relationship with Thelma. In his summing-up at the first trial, O'Leary 'would only say she was an abnormal girl', according to *Truth*.[4] The *Herald* merely reported that he 'hoped he was not doing her an injustice when he referred to her as a subject for commercial photographs' (about which more shortly).[5] At the second trial, according to the *Auckland Star*, O'Leary would only say that Stark had 'formed a particular attachment to Mrs Mareo' and that they had 'the extraordinary habit . . . of getting into bed together at times'.[6] By contrast, as we have seen, Meredith for the Crown chose to add even greater emphasis to the vileness of Mareo's accusation than his predecessor at the first trial, on the assumption of course that it would not be believed.

There was also Thelma's phobia about pregnancy. To our mind this might indicate that she feared or didn't like one or more of the following: sex with men, pregnancy, childbirth, children, or parenthood with all its responsibilities. However, such logic could be reversed. As Johnstone for the Crown argued at the first trial,

> Mareo had said they never lived as man and wife . . . and had further stated that his wife's desires were met by association with women, there being an agreement not to associate as man and wife.
>
> 'And yet,' continued Mr Johnstone, 'according to Mareo, his wife had a great dread of having children.'[7]

Moreover, there was the undisputed fact that, just before she died, Thelma feared that she might actually be pregnant. If it is rather unlikely that she had had sex both with Stark and either Mareo or another man that month, we can only assume that Thelma was indeed in a bad psychological state to believe such a thing. Indeed, taken together with her well-recorded history of recurring trouble with her appendix (and assuming that that was not some other undiagnosed medical condition such as endometriosis), it seems reasonable to assume that she was suffering from one or several psychosomatic or 'hysterical' disorders that were not uncommon amongst certain 'types' of women at the time. The medical historian Edward Shorter has chronicled how 'chronic appendicitis' was an affliction that 'acquired a lively medical following between the 1880s, when appendectomies in general started to be performed, and the 1930s, when the great medical authorities decreed it a non-disease'. Shorter records the tendency of the medical profession during this period to treat the appendix as the 'scapegoat of the abdomen' and as the deemed cause of most, if not all, abdominal discomfort, be it 'troublesome gas in the bowels', constipation or simple indigestion. The surgeons' consequent readiness to remove perfectly healthy organs needlessly perhaps gives Thelma's otherwise apparently neurotic fear of 'an operation' a more rational footing. Nonetheless, the fact that she was plainly susceptible to a diagnosis of 'chronic appendicitis' in the first place perhaps says something about her. For example, a leading London physician in the 1920s noted:

> [T]he subject of the chronic abdomen is usually a woman, generally a spinster, or, if married, childless, and belonging to what are commonly termed – rather ironically nowadays – the 'comfortable' classes. To such a degree, moreover, do her abdominal troubles colour her life and personality that we may conveniently speak of her as an 'abdominal woman'.[8]

Given Thelma's own reported tendency to speak of her great fear both of operations and of pregnancy in the same breath, we can perhaps speculate that the latter was merely symptomatic of her wider 'abdominal neuroses' rather than of a rational belief that she might actually be pregnant.

As for the actual evidence that might indicate that Thelma and Stark were not just sleeping and chatting together in bed, this was rather vague. When Graham was asked at the first trial whether there 'was anything noticeable about' his stepmother and Stark when he discovered them in bed, he replied

> [t]hey were lying close together. Q. Did Mrs Mareo remain calm or appear embarrassed? – She was a bit embarrassed. Q. I think you also felt a bit embarrassed? – Yes. Q. What did you do? – I said I wanted a book and went out. Q. Do you recollect on that occasion you told Mrs Mareo your father would not be home until late? – Yes. Q. Did your father come home late or earlier than he expected? – He came home about ten. . . . Q. When your father came home was everything quiet or was there a row? He went into the bedroom did he not? – Yes. Q. There was a row was there not? – It wasn't a loud one. I didn't hear it. They were talking but I don't know if it was a row or not.[9]

Two days later, according to Dr Walton (whom she saw for a 'nervous condition'), Thelma said that

[h]er husband had made to her some unjust charges – untrue charges – of some kind of perversion. She denied it. Q. She told you did she not that her husband had come home and caught her in bed, undressed, with some other woman? – She told me that. Q. She told you, did she not, that that had happened, but she gave you an explanation of how it happened? X – Yes. Q. What was her explanation? – Her explanation was that she was going to bed with this friend of hers – that this friend of hers used to go to bed with her in the late afternoon or early evening. Her explanation was that she had heard her husband and had popped into bed with nothing on.[10]

Although there may have been something in both Graham's and Dr Walton's testimony to incite prurient imaginations, there was not clear evidence of 'lesbianism'. The testimony of a 17-year-old boy was hardly reliable on the subject of female 'perversion', and his embarrassment upon entering the bedroom of a stepmother he had known for only a few months and her 'bosom friend', both only a few years older than him, was hardly surprising. Similarly, the fact that Thelma had raised Mareo's accusation with Dr Walton could have easily been seen as the kind of confession an actual 'lesbian' would be unlikely to make.

Furthermore, Stark's testimony contradicted both Graham's and Dr Walton's. According to her, Thelma was wearing a black robe and she could not remember Graham coming into the room.[11] Besides, the fact that Thelma and Stark often went to bed together would not necessarily indicate anything other than great friendship. After all, even in the 1930s it was still common for those of the same gender to sleep together, particularly in cramped living conditions. And apparently this was not necessarily restricted to members of the working class. When Betty Mareo testified that Stark and Thelma often shared the same bed, she also said, 'I thought all theatricals were like that.'[12] Since they would often have gone to bed very late, it is hardly surprising that they slept so often during the day. Stark's claim that her 'habit of getting into bed with many of [her] girl friends' was 'nothing unusual' could have been taken at face value.[13]

The Defence also raised what it no doubt hoped might be

some other incriminating facts. Both Betty and Graham remembered seeing some photographs of Stark naked and Graham also remembered seeing 'Thelma looking at them with Freda Stark in her bedroom. I saw them through the door. I wasn't in the room'.[14] However, Stark said at the first trial that these photographs had been 'taken by a well known photographer in Auckland in the presence of his wife' and 'sent to London for exhibition purposes'.[15] Since *Truth* was able to caption photos it reproduced of Stark wearing very little or nothing as 'art studies', it is possible that the association of these photos with some kind of morally elevating notion of Art or Culture would have been a mitigating factor.

But the strongest evidence that Thelma was a 'lesbian' were the three letters given to the police by Mareo to support his accusation. It is quite clear that the author of these letters, a Frenchwoman called Billy who knew Thelma when she lived in Sydney, was a person who, like some of her friends, 'practice[d] the gentle art of Lesbos in [a] modern setting'. In these letters Billy refers to translation by Thelma of Pierre Lou├┐s' *Les Chansons de Bilitis*, a softly pornographic *fin de siècle* imitation of Sappho. However, neither Thelma's translations (which were never found) nor any other were read out in court to enlighten the jurymen about a writer who was obviously not a 'lesbian' in any case. Billy does finish one of her letters by declaring

[w]hat a terrible, crushing thing this antagonism of sex is. It is something that only the strongest or those who love lightly and gently can escape.

I shall never forget that I have held you close in my arms and that I have been proud to think myself
Your lover,
B.

But if this indicates that Thelma and Billy may once have had a sexual relationship (and that is uncertain), it is clear that by the time this letter was written (c.1931) it was over. As Billy also confesses, '[f]or the first time in my life I built dreams around

Eric Mareo as he first appeared in the newspapers.
Independent News Auckland Ltd

Thelma Mareo as the Duchess of Danzig. *Independent News Auckland Ltd*

Above: The Mareo Symphony
Orchestra. *E.A. Aspey*

Below: Thelma Trott, c.1930.
Allan Brownlee

Police shot of Mareo on his arrest. *Eric Mareo Papers*

Greatest Circulation In N.Z. — 81,235 Weekly

N.Z.
*Rangatira
Inquiry,
Page 12.*

N.Z. Truth

*Lawrence's
Great Story,
Page 11.*

WEDNESDAY, FEBRUARY 26, 1936.   (22 PAGES) PRICE 3d.

Dead Woman's Friend In Box At
MAREO TRIAL
Questions by Counsel
For Defence
DOCTOR'S STORY
OF INTERVIEWS

DR. JOHN DREADON, who ordered Mrs. Mareo to hospital.

TWO of the Crown witnesses snapped with the 14x4 Mrs. Mareo—Top: Mrs. Eleanor Brownlee, M.S., Bottom, Miss Freda Stark (left) and Mrs. Mareo.

(From "N.Z. Truth's" Auckland Representative.)

THE INTENSE public interest manifested at the opening has increased during the first week of the trial of the well-known musician, Eric Mareo, aged 44, on a charge of murdering his young wife, Thelma Clarice.

EACH DAY queues of eager people have lined up outside the court before the opening hour, and on occasions an overflow from the women's section has found standing room at the back of the court downstairs. The attendance of the public became greater when the chief witness for the Crown, Freda Stark, friend of the dead woman, and Eleanor Jeanie Brownlee, Mareo's secretary, gave evidence.

NECKS WERE eagerly craned when Mr. H. F. O'Leary, K.C., of Wellington, chief counsel for the defence, rose to cross-examine Miss Stark, some indication of the line his questioning was likely to take having been given by the queries he had already put

Above: *Truth*, 26 February 1936. The picture on the right shows the three women in Mareo's life: Eleanor Brownlee (at the back), Freda Stark (front left), and Thelma Mareo. *Independent News Auckland Ltd*

Right: Freda Stark, also from *Truth*, 26 February 1936. *Independent News Auckland Ltd*

Truth, 18 March 1936. One of the 'art studies' of Freda Stark, referred to in the trials, is in the top right hand corner.
Independent News Auckland Ltd

TS AT MAREO TRIAL

MEMBERS OF THE JURY in the Mareo trial shown outside their hotel. The foreman, Mr. W. K. Jerome, is second from the left in front.

Above: Twelve Angry Men: the first jury. *Truth*, 26 February 1936.
Independent News Auckland Ltd

Below: Freda Stark's epitaph to Thelma. *Truth*, 24 June 1936.
Independent News Auckland Ltd

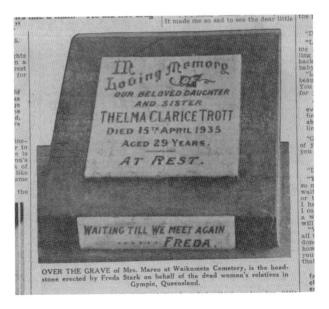

It made me so sad to see the dear little

In Loving Memory

OUR BELOVED DAUGHTER
AND SISTER
THELMA CLARICE TROTT
DIED 15TH APRIL 1935
AGED 29 YEARS.
AT REST.

WAITING TILL WE MEET AGAIN
FREDA.

OVER THE GRAVE of Mrs. Mareo at Waikumete Cemetery, is the headstone erected by Freda Stark on behalf of the dead woman's relatives in Gympie, Queensland.

Left: Mareo leaving Mt Eden gaol. *Independent News Auckland Ltd*

Below: His new dentures. *Independent News Auckland Ltd*

a woman; and it would seem I have made a very proper fool of myself . . . I do not blame you for the fact that you cannot love me.' Perhaps Thelma could not love Billy because of her own inhibitions about lesbianism. After all, Billy notes that while the charges of obscenity against the Australian writer Norman Lindsay had just been 'dropped', '[t]here is a breeze of Puritanism blowing all over Australia' and in another letter that Thelma had been '[s]urprised' that she had written about

> 'forbidden' subjects with her. Of course in the English conception of life they are tabu, sinful, unclean; if I think them healthy and fascinating, you must show me I am wrong, and don't think it is a lack of respect I have for you, not at all, if I write to you about painting, literature, poetry, you will think I try to insult you, if you want to understand me take off you monalistic [sic] glasses and look at with your intellectual and esthetignes [sic] ones; of course you can answer, put the monalistic glasses on yourself, well I tried, and everything became ugly . . . I was surprised at the excessive popularity of Freud in English-speaking countries; it is because there is an unhealthy amount of sex repression which manifests itself by an exaggerated sentimentalism before. Do you know how D. H. Lawrence gave a definition of chastity: Purity, with a dirty little secret. . . . In France, it is quite different, exactly the opposite, that is why very few French women and girls are neurotic, if you ask me why.[16]

Thus, even allowing for the fact that a rejected lover is not a very reliable judge of such matters, Thelma is represented as someone hardly at ease with the 'vice' of 'lesbianism'. Billy might castigate Thelma for her 'Puritanism', but presumably the jurymen would have thought that in such circumstances this was a commendable trait.

Moreover, while it might be clear to us what Billy means by 'the gentle art of Lesbos', this is never spelled out in the letters, and we can assume that these jurymen might have been somewhat mystified. After all, at the first trial the Crown Prosecutor asked Thelma's GP, Dr Walton, '[i]s it not a fact that

Lesbianism is not a precise term? Is it a precise term or a general term referring to relations between women which may be innocuous?', and Dr Walton replied rather tentatively that 'I think it refers really to gratification of sexual feelings between women'.[17] However, a doctor could be expected to know about something which was, as we shall soon see, commonly regarded as a medical condition. In contrast, the senior police officer involved with the investigation testified that until this case he had 'not know[n] the word "Lesbian" or its meaning',[18] and Stark claimed that she 'did not know what the term "Lesbian" meant' when she first heard Mareo use the word.[19] This is quite plausible since at the first trial she never used the word 'lesbian', whereas at the second, after she had become acquainted with the term, she used it on several occasions.

Julie Glamuzina and Alison Laurie recount the anecdote about Sonja Davies in the mid-1940s overhearing a New Zealand nurse asking another, '[W]hat are lesbians?' and another wondering, '[I]s it a political party?'[20] As they observe, '[f]or some lesbians the reports of the Parker-Hulme case [the sensational trial of two female teenagers for the murder of one of their mothers in Christchurch in 1954] were their first affirmation that there *were* other lesbians'.[21]

But neither had the term 'lesbian' become common currency outside New Zealand. It was not until the late nineteenth century that 'lesbian' referred to anyone other than an inhabitant of the Greek island of Lesbos, about half of whom in recent times have been men. Even the so called 'sexologists' of the late nineteenth and early twentieth centuries, men such as Karl Heinrich Ulrichs, Richard von Krafft-Ebing and Magnus Hirschfeld in Germany, and Havelock Ellis and Edward Carpenter in Britain, preferred to call male and female 'homosexuals' (itself a word first used only in 1869), 'inverts' or 'Uranians', and their gender an 'intermediate' or 'third' sex. Female homosexuals were also sometimes called 'sapphists'. And in her letter to O'Leary (but not in her testimony), Mrs Irene Riano wrote that it 'was fairly well known in the company and other theatrical circles' in Australia that Thelma was a 'bi-sexual subject'.[22] Then as now, nomenclature was clearly in a process of change.

Nevertheless, despite such terminological uncertainty, it seems that a reasonably simple concept of male and female homosexual identity was widespread in most European countries by the latter part of the nineteenth century. Before then, as Jeffrey Weeks explains,

> [t]he law was directed [in Britain as in most other countries] against a series of sexual acts, not a particular type of person. There was no concept of the homosexual in law, and homosexuality was regarded not as a particular attribute of a certain type of person but as a potential in all sinful creatures.[23]

But by the end of the nineteenth century a 'homosexual' was generally defined not as someone who engaged in sexual acts with someone of the same gender but as someone who adopted the gender role or behaviour of the opposite 'sex'. For example, a study of American sailors just before the First World War has established that the men who committed various sexual acts with effeminate male prostitutes did not think of themselves as homosexual.[24] The concept of homosexuality as a form of gender inversion is usually accredited to the late nineteenth-century sexologists but this study suggests that the medical model of homosexuality may have been derived from popular conceptions of homosexuality, rather than the other way around. In any case, the concept of gender inversion also applied to female homosexuals, even though lesbianism was ignored by the criminal codes.[25]

Of course, such a narrow concept could hardly describe the actual lives of non-heterosexual men and women. Nevertheless, the nature of Stark and Thelma's relationship, or for that matter the actual lives of other 'lesbians' during the 1930s, is not our concern. What is at issue is the public perception of 'lesbianism'. Although little is known about either popular conceptions or the medical model of homosexuality in New Zealand during the first decades of the century, there is no reason to suppose that New Zealand was much different from any other Western country. The work of the sexologists was certainly widely available: Stevan Eldred-Grigg records that in 1908 the Attorney-General recommended that other Members of Parliament read *The Evolution of Sex*, one of the more influential works of sexology, and in 1911 a Legislative Counsellor described Havelock Ellis as 'an authority which cannot be disputed'.[26]

As far as the trials are concerned, it seems that 'lesbianism' was certainly considered to be some kind of medical condition. Although Thelma was visiting Dr Walton because of her 'nerves', the fact that she raised the issue with him (if only to deny it emphatically) indicates that she might have believed that it was the kind of 'condition' about which a doctor should be informed. Certainly, it was assumed during the trials that Dr Walton could be asked about lesbianism simply because he was a doctor. Furthermore, only five years after the trials, Sir William Willcox, who had been asked to give an opinion on the medical evidence presented at the trial, came to the conclusion that Thelma had administered the veronal to herself and that she 'was suffering from abnormal sexuality (homosexuality or lesbianism). This condition is commonly associated with addiction to drugs like Barbitone [or veronal] and to alcoholic excess.'[27] Although Dr P.P. Lynch, a consulting pathologist to the Wellington Hospital and an Examiner in Pathology at the University of New Zealand, disagreed with Sir William's conclusions and in particular his 'statement that Thelma Mareo's abnormal sexual life was one which is commonly associated with addiction to drugs', he did not deny that there was a causal connection between 'lesbianism' and drug addiction, merely saying that Sir William's statement was 'a generalisation which is comparable to a declaration that many criminals are either drug addicts or alcoholics'.[28] (In fact, the association of lesbianism with alcoholism can be traced back to Ellis's *Sexual Inversion*, published in 1897, where the case history of an unnamed woman usually assumed to be his wife, Edith Lees, begins by mentioning that '[h]er grandfather drank; her father was eccentric and hypochondriacal, and suffered from obsessions'.[29] Even as late as the early 1960s, a New Zealand mental health specialist referring to 'sociopathic personality disturbance' could mention in the same phrase 'alcoholism, drug addiction, and sexual deviations'.[30])

However, the strongest evidence that at least some of the protagonists were thinking about lesbianism in ways similar to the sexologists was the testimony of Mrs Irene Riano. She remembered a discussion with Thelma in Melbourne

> regarding certain books. One was the *Unlit Lamp*, another *The Well of Loneliness*, and there was a third one but I can't remember its name. The two I have mentioned are by Radclyffe Hall. These books dealt with the life of a Lesbian. I had discussed these books with Thelma.[31]

Radclyffe Hall's *The Well of Loneliness* had been the object of a sensational British censorship trial in 1928, subsequently becoming the world's best-known 'lesbian novel' and a byword for female 'perversion'. The fact that Irene Riano could mention *The Well of Loneliness* in a New Zealand courtroom (perhaps as a more subtle way of suggesting that Thelma was a 'bi-sexual subject') suggests that she believed that those present would at least have heard about the trial, even though the novel had been banned in New Zealand. Significantly, the novel's representation of female homosexuals accorded closely with the medical model disseminated by the sexologists. Hall's lesbian characters or 'inverts', including its heroine, the aristocratic and mannish Stephen Gordon, were in part modelled on some of the case studies in Ellis's *Sexual Inversion*; Ellis himself wrote an introduction to the book; and its author defended the novel with the claim that her conception of 'inversion' had behind it 'the weight of most of the finest psychological opinion'.[32] Although they were not convinced of the book's literary value, writers such as Virginia Woolf and E.M. Forster wrote in support of *The Well of Loneliness* on the assumption that the putative artistic merits of the novel would make the public more tolerant of its subject matter. Although she was no literary critic, this was also the tactic adopted by Irene Riano at the second Mareo trial. As she told the Auckland courtroom, Hall's two novels were

> fine works well written and not in any way indecent or vulgar. They were almost classical. I had myself read them right through with an appreciation of the tragedy. I would not think anything of anybody who had also read them with appreciation.[33]

But neither Thelma nor Stark resembled an 'invert', a type defined by Hall and the sexologists as a genitally female person who adopted the male gender role. Stark was about five feet tall and Thelma only one or two inches taller; they were both physically light, and conventionally feminine in appearance – as one might expect of a chorus girl and an actress. Photographs of both women were reproduced in nearly all the newspapers, particular favourites being a publicity portrait of Thelma resplendent in evening dress and jewels when she was the leading lady of *The Duchess of Danzig*, and various 'art' shots of Stark thinly clad or naked. Thelma was habitually described as 'beautiful' and 'glamorous' while the more athletic Stark appeared '[t]o the inquisitive who crowded the court . . . what she is in person – petite, lissome, and possessed of a poise developed largely from her training as a dancer and her experience on the stage'.[34]

The contrast between these women and Hall – who often appeared in the English papers posed like a gentleman, wearing a monocle, short hair and black tie, and with a cigarette lodged between the knuckles rather than the tips of the fingers – could not have been more striking. Nor would Thelma and Freda have resembled home-grown 'inverts' such as 'Boy' Bertha from Hokitika (who was arrested in 1906 in Sydney while dressed as a man), or Amy Bock (imprisoned for fraud in 1909 for marrying a woman who thought she was a man), or the cross-dressing Wellingtonian Eugenia Falleni (who was arrested in the 1920s for the murder of 'his' wife), or Deresley Morton (who married a woman and died in California in 1929).[35] Of course, there were many more women who might today be considered 'homosexual' or 'lesbian' (even assuming that such terms can be defined), but, again, it is only the largely heterosexual public's perception of 'lesbians' that is relevant. Perhaps the juries and some members of the public interested in the case did think it possible that Thelma and Stark were involved in some kind of sexual relationship, but this would not necessarily have meant that they believed they were 'lesbians'. If 'lesbians' were 'inverts' then the sexual partner of an 'invert' would not strictly be a 'lesbian' and two 'femmes' (to use an anachronistic term) who engaged in some kind of sexual activity would simply be 'normal', or heterosexual, women committing 'immoral' acts. In D.H. Lawrence's *The Rainbow*, for example, which was largely written just before the First World War, one of the heroines, Ursula, has a brief sexual relationship with her female teacher, and yet Lawrence seems in no doubt that both women are essentially heterosexual.

But if the juries did not believe that Thelma and Stark's relationship corresponded with the medical model of 'lesbianism', what might they have thought about their friendship? According to the American historian Lillian Faderman,

> [i]t was still possible in the early twentieth century for some women to vow great love for each other, sleep together, see themselves as life mates, perhaps even make love, and yet have no idea that their relationship was what the sexologists were now considering 'inverted' and 'abnormal.' Such naiveté was possible for women who came out of the nineteenth-century tradition of romantic friendship and were steeped in its literature. Even had they been exposed to the writings of the sexologists, which were by now being slowly disseminated in America, they might have been unable to recognise themselves and their relationships in those medical descriptions.[36]

These 'romantic friendships' – which included schoolgirl 'crushes' in England, 'smashing' between American college students, and 'Boston marriages' between mature women – were not only tolerated by men but in many cases strongly valorised. For example, Faderman begins her history of twentieth-century American lesbianism by citing the following description of a 'female friendship' between 'maiden ladies' by the mid-nineteenth-century author William Cullen Bryant:

> [I]n their youthful days, they took each other as companions for life, and this union, no less sacred to them than the tie of marriage, has subsisted, in uninterrupted harmony, for 40 years, during which they have shared each others' occupations and pleasures and works of charity while in health, and watched over each other tenderly in sickness. . . . They slept on the same pillow and had a common purse, and adopted each other's relations, and . . . I would tell you of their dwelling, encircled with roses, . . . and I would speak of the friendly attentions which their neighbours, people of kind hearts and simple manners, seem to take pleasure in bestowing upon them.[37]

Such romantic friendships reached their heyday around the turn of the century, partly because of increased educational opportunities for women. Faderman records that over a third of the American college population in 1880 were women and between 1880 and 1900 fifty per cent of these women remained single compared to ten per cent for the general population.[38]

There is no reason to suspect that such romantic friendships did not exist in New Zealand as well as in Britain. Although much research is still to be done on the institution of romantic friendship in New Zealand, it seems writers such as Jane Mander, Margaret Escott, Ngaio Marsh and Ursula Bethell, the expatriate painter Frances Hodgkins, and the mountain climber Freda Du Faur, were involved in such friendships. Whether or not these relationships were also sexual does not concern us because they were all perceived at the time as socially acceptable. Although Du Faur and her partner would now be described as a 'lesbian' couple, for example, they were comfortable with the public perception of their relationship as a kind of romantic friendship, but were later made extremely uncomfortable by the impact of the work of the sexologists.[39]

Certainly it is the case that *Truth* represented Thelma and Stark's relationship in accordance with the conventions of a romantic friendship. An interview Stark gave to that paper after the first trial, for example, has all the classic features of popular romance. It begins with Stark at home, '[a] hint of wistfulness frequently shading her eyes', remembering how she first met Thelma after being employed as a replacement for an injured dancer. The scene – Hamilton, a place nostalgically revisited by Freda after Thelma's death – and the action – a dancer being 'thrown above her partner's head into a [badly executed] splits on the floor' – may not sound particularly romantic, but *Truth* insists that it is one of the 'almost unbelievable strands' of 'a story that seems to have sprung from out of the covers of fiction'. Stark then remembers the life and accomplishments of her beloved: the youngest of a family of six from Queensland, Thelma was

> educated at the Gympie Convent. . . . won her junior and senior national scholarships . . . became a B.A. at the age of twenty. . . . was a brilliant musician, being able to play the piano, violin and mandolin. . . . possessed a beautiful voice . . . was a talented actress. . . . painted many beautiful landscape scenes and studies of people, and executed some excellent pastel drawings. . . . designed and made all her own clothes. . . . was a good stenographer. . . . earned good money while she was on the stage, being always one of the principals in whatever company she was in. . . . [kept] herself well dressed and [sent] money home to her mother every fortnight the eight or nine years that she worked on the stage.

Despite these accomplishments, Stark confesses, 'I was her only close friend'. She concludes her interview by explaining

> that she ascertained the address of Thelma's parents after her friend's death through finding a letter from Gympie in the lining of Thelma's coat.
> It was some time before she could bring herself to write to her dead friend's mother, but at last she did and she had never regretted doing it.[40]

From Milton's 'Lycidas' through Tennyson's 'In Memoriam'

to the contemporary elegies of popular romance, the conventions remain much the same: a friend or lover grieves for a remarkable person tragically brought down in the prime of life, remembers the miraculous circumstances of their meeting and brief life together, and then vows to perpetuate their memory. And the mourning lover is a less remarkable person than the beloved. Stark is a chorus girl and the daughter of a bootmaker and therefore someone with whom ordinary New Zealanders can empathise, whereas Thelma the leading lady was a BA and from the unfortunately named but nevertheless suitably distant town of Gympie, Queensland. Theirs was a romance that spanned not only the classes but the Tasman Sea. It was soon after this interview that Stark had inscribed on Thelma's headstone the words 'Waiting Till We Meet Again . . . Freda'.

The fact that *Truth* represented the women's relationship in romantic rather than medical terms might suggest that New Zealand lagged somewhat behind the United States and Britain in terms of sexual mores. As Faderman argues,

> [w]ith the growing popularity of sexology in the 1920s (particularly through the fashionableness of Freud and psychoanalysis), as well as the publication of Radclyffe Hall's *succès de scandale*, *The Well of Loneliness* in 1928, and the emergence in the 1920s of a somewhat visible homosexual subculture in both Europe and America, it became virtually impossible for two women to enjoy intensely close relationships and not be suspected of lesbianism.[41]

However, one imagines that even amongst the intelligentsias of Boston, New York, Paris and London there was a period of transition. And if amongst such people it had become 'virtually impossible' by the mid-1930s to believe in romantic friendships between women, presumably that was not the case everywhere else and amongst those who were not from either the intelligentsia or bohemia. Presumably in places where there was at most a barely 'visible homosexual subculture', such as Auckland, people were becoming increasingly aware of 'medical'

notions of 'sexual inversion' but could still believe that women
such as Stark and Thelma were 'merely' 'bosom friends'. A guilty
verdict would therefore have told a reassuring story about the
absence of sexual 'deviancy' in New Zealand while confirming
what had always been suspected of people such as the French.
By pronouncing Mareo guilty the juries were in a sense attempting to arrest what, from their point of view, would have been a
troubling process of historical change. Given how ideologically
charged concepts of sexuality must have been at this time (or
for that matter anywhere and at any time), it is not surprising
that the all-male juries chose to find Mareo guilty and therefore
tell a reassuring story about virtuous women physically and
spiritually assaulted by a man of uncertain background and
profession. The alternative would have implied that 'lesbians'
were 'here' rather than 'elsewhere'.

However, it is also possible that the jurymen knew at some
level that Thelma and Stark were not just friends but were able
to ignore or suppress such knowledge. No doubt many people
did suspect that women involved in romantic friendships did
indulge in 'immoral' activities of one kind or another but such
women did not, at least publicly, challenge conventional notions
of femininity or conventional gender roles. On the other hand,
women such as Radclyffe Hall did. As long as 'lesbian' love
does not dare to speak its name – to adapt Oscar Wilde – it
remains socially unthreatening. Thus, while even Billy uses the
word 'sex' on several occasions when she writes about sexual
love between women, it is always in euphemistic terms and
accompanied by a barrage of literary and artistic references:

> Our Christian morality is so opposite to the Greek morality,
> and, I must say, the morality of the people who built the
> Acropale, wrote Oedipus rex and scupt the Parthenon freize,
> who give Socrate and Plato to the world, is good for me.[42]

If most people knew what such references to the Greeks really
meant they could hardly object since, to use Matthew Arnold's
terms, Culture was Hellenic as well as Hebraic. By not resorting

to euphemism or ambiguous references to the Greeks, Mareo was attempting, as a much later generation would say, to 'out' Thelma. By pronouncing him guilty the juries were in a sense either denying the existence of lesbianism in New Zealand or keeping it safely closeted.

CHAPTER SIX

A Pharmakon, a Pharmakos and a Pure Woman

I can't help it, she said, pulling a long face.
It's them pills I took to bring it off, she said.
(She's had five already and nearly died of young George.)
You are a proper fool, I said.
Well, if Albert won't leave you alone, there it is, I said.
What you get married for if you don't want children?
—T.S. Eliot, *The Waste Land* (1922)

MUCH OF THE MEDICAL testimony during the trials would have stood in stark contrast to this tale of romantic friendship. Not only did the juries hear how the comatose Thelma was supported to the lavatory and then later removed from her urine and menstrual-blood-soaked bedclothes to be taken to hospital, but they had to sit through what must have been for lay people some rather disturbing scientific testimony. The government analyst, Griffin, began by testifying that

On 16th April 1935 I received from Det. Serg. Meiklejohn 3 jars containing certain parts of a human body, parts of the brain, liver, spleen, 2 kidneys, stomach and contents. The liver spleen and kidneys were in one jar, and the others in separate jars. I also received 3 test tubes containing urine taken from body and a bottle of urine (Ex. 20) labelled 'Mrs T. Mareo. Urine 15/4/35'. Another bottle Ex. 19 labelled 'Stomach lavage. Mrs Thelma Mareo'.[1]

If the juries had only known, they would have recognised that such testimony resembled some of the 'found poems' or objets trouvées then being 'written' by the European avant-garde. But this was neither Paris nor London and, as Griffin explained, he was given 2 lbs of brain. I first put it through the mincer machine – the whole 2 lbs – It is probably a superior type of household mincer. It is thoroughly minced up and goes through a mesh of a 1/16th of an inch. It is then mixed, which is done with a spoon in a jar, thoroughly. This is the method always used in treating samples, according to standard textbooks. Having got my mixture, I took 1 lb out of the 2 lbs. I adopted the same performance with the case of the other organs where I did not have the whole amount. Except in case of the stomach lining, where I took the whole of it.[2]

At any time the mincing of parts of a woman's body according to some bizarre medical recipe by 'a superior type of household mincer' would be, despite its necessity, repellent for most people. This was probably especially the case during the 1930s when female identity was so strongly linked to notions of sexual and physical purity. Although the cults of domesticity and mother-hood that derived from, or helped produce, such notions were prevalent in other Western societies, there is reason to suspect that they were particularly strong in New Zealand. After all, in comparison to most other Western countries, Pakeha New Zealand had a stronger middle class and a higher proportion of people from the evangelical denominations, both of which have been particularly susceptible to the kinds of discourses of female purity that emerged from about the eighteenth century onwards.[3] The success of the 1890s feminist movement in gaining the vote for women before anywhere else in the world is one sign of the historical strength of such discourses. As Phillida Bunkle has shown, its main organisation, the Women's Christian Temper-ance Union, promulgated a world view that opposed female purity to dangerous 'male sexual energy'.[4] Thus, from the 1880s onwards, according to Erik Olssen,

> [A] small group of Protestant activists spelt out a new vision of an alcohol-free society from which the sexual double standard had been eradicated. As part of the new emphasis on purity, the home was elevated into an article of religious faith and Mother was reinvented as its guardian angel. The conjugal family became *the* family.[5]

Such a vision was probably largely unaffected by either the challenge to traditional gender roles that occurred in Britain following the influx of women into the workforce during the Great War or by any kind of postwar sexual revolution.[6] Significantly, it was in these decades that Truby King's Plunket Society partly succeeded in medicalising the 'vocation' of motherhood, thereby severely narrowing whatever radical potential the cult of female purity once had.[7] Thus, in the year of the Mareo trials the *Women's Weekly* was able to proclaim that the New Zealand wife and mother was the 'Prime Minister' of her 'home'.[8]

In such a context the poisoning of a youngish wife by her much older cosmopolitan husband would probably have appeared especially disturbing. Many already regarded poisoners as somehow worse than other types of murderers. Meredith (the Crown Prosecutor), for example, told the second jury that '[a] poisoning case was the most insidious form of murder'.[9] Somewhat later, an Attorney-General of New Zealand would explain that '[a]gainst open assault a man may defend himself. Against the poisoner he has no defence. The victim generally receives the poison from the hands of one they trust and love, and the only protection is the certainty of conviction and punishment'. Meredith would write in a book of legal reminiscences that 'those . . . words still stand true for most cases of poisoning'.[10] Thus, a murderer who literally poisoned a 'pure' woman such as Thelma would have been regarded as an especially sinister figure.

Moreover, this particular murderer had not used a simple poison but a drug, and that at a time when there was a growing concern about such substances. Whereas for the ancient Greeks the word *pharmakos* had meant both medicine and poison, the nearest equivalent in English, 'drug', did not acquire such ambiguity until a handful of years before the Mareo trials. As one historian has pointed out in another context, 'drug' was defined in the first edition of the *Oxford English Dictionary* published in 1897 as only '[a]n original, simple medicinal substance, organic or inorganic, whether used by itself in its natural condition or prepared by art, or as an ingredient in a medicine or medicament', and only by the time of the publication of the 1910 edition of the *Encyclopedia Britannica* is there a record of the noun being 'often used synonymously for narcotics or poisonous substances', as well as for medicine.[11]

Accordingly, during the first two decades of the century there were various international conventions on the issue of controlling the international drug trade. In response to one of these at The Hague in 1925, the New Zealand Government passed the Dangerous Drugs Act of 1927, regulating the exportation and importation of drugs such as opium, morphine, cocaine and cannabis and restricting their manufacture and sale. However, other dangerous drugs were still able to circulate too freely, at least according to Robin Hyde writing for the *New Zealand Observer* in July of 1932. A drug user herself (her supplier was a Queen Street pharmacist whom she referred to as Father Time and the Little Grey Man), Hyde reports that 'the depression has caused increased nervous strain, and has weakened the resistance of men and women who a few years ago would have shunned' drugs such as cocaine and morphine. However,

> [v]eronal, the sleep-producing drug that is much in the public eye just now, is not yet down on New Zealand's black list of dangerous drugs, but it has been the cause of so many recent tragedies that the New Zealand Pharmacy Board is moving in the direction of having it so listed.
>
> Every chemist in New Zealand has reason to know and fear the effect of veronal when it is rashly used, or administered by people who do not realise its deadly power. The Auckland district, in particular, has in the last few months acquired a veronal death-roll of which it cannot be proud. A young married woman died recently of an overdose: more recently still, in the north, a promising young medical man died from the same tragic cause.[12]

But veronal was not just unintentionally misused. For some years it had been a popular method of suicide, particularly amongst the literati. Both Eugene O'Neill (in 1912) and Virginia Woolf (in 1913), for example, had made serious attempts at dispatching themselves in this way; the latter, incidentally, only surviving after having a dose pumped from her stomach of exactly the amount which allegedly killed Thelma. To guard against such misuse, the Poisons Act of 1934 came into force about two weeks before Thelma's death, ensuring that New Zealanders could no longer freely acquire certain drugs, including veronal, without a medical prescription, and as a consequence Mareo felt compelled to stock up.[13]

As the social significance of many drugs changed, so did the image of the person using them. During the same period, according to the historian referred to above, 'the image of the addict changed, from that of a middle-class victim accidentally addicted through medicinal use to that of a criminal or otherwise deviant individual who had turned to drugs for purely recreational reasons'.[14] As Mareo's supporter, Melville Harcourt, explained,

> when, during the course of the trial, it was revealed that Eric Mareo was a drug addict, the prejudice against him tightened considerably. You see, to those honest citizens from whom juries are selected there is something heinous about the very word 'drug' once it has been detached from its medical associations; they instinctively connect it with crime (it's useless, in contradiction, to cite some of the most luminous figures in literature that were addicts but assuredly not criminals), and there's no question that the fact that Eric Mareo was a self-confessed addict enormously depreciated his chances of an acquittal.[15]

But not only had Mareo supposedly murdered his talented wife with an apparently medicinal drug disguised in a cup of milk redolent with childhood associations, in the apparent safety of a suburban, middle-class home, he had also been posing as a dutiful and concerned husband. It was not just that his murder weapon of choice was a kind of *pharmakos* but that he was a kind of *pharmakon*, a word related to *pharmakos* that refers to a Greek citizen who is chosen to be a scapegoat. Like the *pharmakon*, Mareo was both a valued member of his community and yet also by virtue of his unusual profession outside ordinary society. He spoke with an English accent and hailed from Britain at a time when Aucklanders would have thought of themselves as British, and yet he had changed his Germanic name to something that would have sounded vaguely Italian. Some sociologists have argued that it is not so much the strangeness or difference of certain social groups that produces prejudice as their ambiguous or ambivalent characteristics.[16] We have suggested that Mareo's profession and manner would have provoked resentment, but there is also reason to suspect that it was his uncertain nationality and past that provoked suspicion. Like the Germans who in pre-WWI spy fiction posed as normal Englishmen, the Jews who looked just like gentiles in postwar antisemitic discourse, or, for that matter, Bela Lugosi's famous depiction in the 1931 film of Count Dracula as a displaced European aristocrat attired in black tie searching for fresh game and resembling the Auckland musician, Mareo was someone pretending to be something he wasn't. After the trials, the *Observer* published an article called, significantly, 'Mareo the Enigma', and even Harcourt conceded that

> [M]oody and gay, passionate and fickle, charming and self-centred, [Mareo] could be all these; there was a protean quality about his personality that often puzzled even his friends and admirers.[17]

Like the drug with which he had poisoned Thelma, Mareo appeared to be a dangerous character precisely because of his ambiguous qualities.

Even the kinds of traits that we now admire would have confused many of the conventional social roles of the time. It seems, for example, that while he did most of the housework, this made him a dubious figure, at least according to a woman called Helen Frances Blagrove, the Mareos' landlady before they moved to Tenterden Avenue. She felt compelled to inform the Minister of Justice, in an unsolicited letter, that Mareo was 'a most funny and peculiar man', in part because he 'cleaned the windows for his wife [and] did most of the housework'.[18] It also appears that Mareo was an affectionate father whose devotion to his children was warmly returned. While New Zealand fathers were expected to be just as devoted to their children, most would not have spent anywhere near as much time looking after them. Nor of course would most New Zealand fathers have needed to have changed their home and country of residence so many times.

But why did Thelma's lack of interest in housework and her inability to get on with Betty not raise suspicions about her character? As O'Leary pointed out in his final address to the jury at the first trial, not only was Thelma a 'stepmother who knew little of how to care for boys', but she was an 'extremely nervous type' 'not suited to housework'.[19] However, a younger woman married to a man who has children from some previous and rather dubious relationship is presumably not expected to display the usual maternal qualities. And, as for the fact that Thelma was clearly lacking a strong housework ethic, it seems that her 'bosom friend' was more than able to compensate. In an interview with Stark after the first trial, *Truth* did claim that Thelma had done 'her household duties', coached Graham for his matriculation exams and taught him the violin; but as though aware that it might be stretching credulity the paper dwelled largely on the domestic accomplishments of Stark. Her home, it discovers,

> [I]s neat and comfortably-furnished, redolent of good house-keeping. The secret of that is simple. Freda's mother impresses as jolly and capable, and the girl – for Freda is essentially girlish in many of her ways – is similarly possessed of domestic ability. She performs her share of the household duties. Indeed, there were occasions during her friendship with Mrs Mareo that she could not find time to call on her actress friend, because there were tasks to be done at home.[20]

Of course Stark was also a 'theatrical' and therefore someone potentially as beyond the pale as Mareo. However, it was probably more socially acceptable for a woman to be a 'theatrical' than a man, even though the entertainment world was undoubtedly male-dominated. As we have seen, the *Herald*'s music critic certainly believed that most people thought there was something 'unmanly' about being a musician, and, while a musical career was hardly a conventional choice for most women, it presumably represented less of a threat to their sexual identity. True, the realm of entertainment and high culture was within neither the public nor private spheres, in whose environs dwelt, respectively, such middle-class figures as the Breadwinner and the Angel of the House. The art gallery, concert or music hall, cinema and literary salon were situated within neither the home nor the workplace. However, books were read, music heard and photographs viewed in the home but virtually never in the workplace. As we have seen, in a society in which 'art' was both highly valued and viewed with hostility, it would be far easier for a woman to embody its positive aspects and a man its negative than vice versa.

Thus, while at the first trial O'Leary had asked Dr Walton whether Thelma was 'of an artistic temperament', to which the doctor answered '[y]ou might put it that way',[21] he did not raise this issue at the second trial, and, apart from this brief exchange, Thelma's occupation of 'theatrical' was never directly associated with any kind of 'nervous' condition, despite the many obvious difficulties of her professional life. On the contrary, she was virtually never described in any of the newspapers without adjectives such as 'talented' and 'accomplished'. Although this was no doubt largely to bring out the tragedy of her death, it also creates the impression that such a woman could have had no reason either to kill herself or to place her life in jeopardy.

In contrast, the newspapers were unable to refer to Mareo's (usually 'diabolical') crime without also mentioning his 'brilliance'. Again, the main purpose of this contrast is to highlight the extraordinarily dramatic nature of his fall, but the implication is that there might be some kind of connection between artistic 'brilliance' and criminality. Harcourt claimed in his book about the trials that '[t]here are "types" whom it's almost impossible to associate with certain crimes', such as 'the genuine artist, the true dilettante, [who] will recoil from the callous, protracted business of poisoning'.[22] But the fact that he begins the section of his book specifically devoted to a defence of Mareo by making this point suggests that he might have been countering a popular belief – which has undoubtedly existed in European societies since the Romantics – that the 'artist' might be more prone than others to 'crime'. Certainly, the Controller-General of Prisons denied Harcourt's claim, pointing out that '[m]any of the most callous and diabolical murderers were supposedly gentle and refined', and then giving a list of some of the more famous refined and cultivated poisoners.[23] And, in response to the *Observer* article about the 'complex and contradictory aspects' of 'Mareo the Enigma', a correspondent arguing against the death penalty nevertheless claimed that there is a 'strong affinity' between the 'super-normal' or 'abnormal', of whom presumably the artistic Mareo is an example, and the insane and criminals.[24] Thus, while 'theatricals' and their families were different from 'ordinary' New Zealanders by virtue of their artistic qualities, they might be either 'better' or 'worse'. Being outside 'normal' society is ambiguous, but at least Thelma encapsulated only its 'good' aspects and Mareo its 'bad'.

Similarly, while the purchase and use of Morgan's drugs might have by the conventional standards of the time reflected poorly on both husband and wife, it seems that it largely indicated, at least to the juries, only Mareo's dubious moral standards. One would have thought that a married woman with a phobia of pregnancy would be an unlikely candidate for Angel of the House. Moreover, since the onset of the Depression birth rates had fallen and the incidence of abortion increased. Indeed, in the same year as the Mareo trials the new Labour government initiated an Inquiry into Abortion that called on 'the womanhood of New Zealand . . . to consider the grave physical and moral dangers, not to speak of the dangers of race suicide' consequent upon any form of birth control.[25] However, at a time of economic hardship it was not difficult for many to condone some forms of birth control, without questioning the higher calling of motherhood. The writer, feminist and family planning advocate, Elsie Locke, told the Inquiry that more than a half of women had attempted some kind of abortion during their married lives, and others argued that some form of birth control would even allow for better childrearing practices. But, more importantly, according to historian Barbara Brookes, although '[i]t was technically illegal to abort oneself . . . this section of the law was generally regarded as a dead letter'.[26] Thus, while Thelma was an unlikely Angel of the House, there may have been some sympathy, at least amongst women, for her reluctance to have children. Moreover, there would have been some hostility towards the man who was (presumably) responsible for her (hypothetical) condition, and who had actually procured the drug from another man. Except for his alleged refusal to call a doctor, Mareo was always active in contrast to the invariably supine Thelma. If the juries were able to dispel doubts about the latter's sexuality, then they would not have had much problem dealing with her misapprehensions about motherhood when there were already two young adults to support and uncertain employment.

Thus, while Thelma had actually been a heavy-drinking, drug-taking 'theatrical' or 'bohemian', it would not have been difficult for the juries to imagine that a much older cosmopolitan womaniser with a dubious past and an uncertain nationality had poisoned the body and then the reputation of a virtuous woman. In fact, the virtuous woman's mother had already written this story. In a series of letters written to Stark just before the first trial, Thelma's mother implored her daughter's friend to help send Mareo to the gallows. Mrs Trott's first letter reads:

My Dear Miss Stark,
You have not the remotest idea the comfort your letter has given me.

I have longed for someone to write and say they knew my little girl. Do not be afraid to tell me all you know. My faith in God will help me over it all, and my darling forever near me. I shall never forget the week of his arrest. Thelma hovers around me day and night. I often wonder if she got my letter saying how worried I was over my dream.

I saw the darling on a ladder that almost reached Heaven. She awoke and was singing, and he was groveling somewhere below. I remember Thelma saying she was going to Freda to do some sewing.

Was the little soul happy? I am told she kept all her sorrows always from me . . . I will pray to bring the fiend to justice.

Oh, Miss Stark, to think of a child so tenderly brought up and highly educated, not a shadow to cross her path. Thank God she spent the best years of her life in happiness.

Do the people over there believe Thelma would take her life? Never.

I will look forward to your letters as though you were dear little Thelma. Love from both . . .[27]

About a week later she also wrote

My Dear Miss Stark,
. . . You have been in my thoughts day and night. It must have been a trying ordeal for you. You can rest assured we will ever remember you for defending our beloved daughter.

If all the world came and told me my little daughter Thelma was a drunkard I would tell them to go and lie no more. If a glass of wine or such like terms one a drunkard, well the rest of the world are such . . .

Thelma was the essence of refinement. He was not even fit for her to wipe her shoes on. They say love is blind. I am sure of it in Thelma's case. Oh, it makes me ill to think of it; a girl brought up, educated like Thelma was, to live under the same roof with such a criminal.

Do you know if he paid for the burial? It was just like burying a dog as far as he was concerned. If not paid for, I hope they can claim the insurance . . .

Can you imagine Thelma spending money on drink, and save as she did, and send money home every fortnight the years she was away? Always two letters a week. I asked her not to send any more money about six months before she died, as I read between the lines.

I hope you will be able to understand this scribble. My eyes are very bad tonight. Goodbye love . . .[28]

In fairness to Mrs Trott, it should be pointed out that she was clearly devastated by her daughter's death. Thelma sent her money regularly, presumably because she and her husband Henry, a Yorkshire-born carpenter who died in 1949, no longer had an income. Moreover, Thelma, her youngest child, was born when she was forty-one. Her beautiful, talented and university-educated daughter must have been the light of her life. Nevertheless, Mrs Trott's letters reduce the tragedy of her daughter's life to a kind of Victorian melodrama about female purity assailed by male depravity. Thelma is on a 'ladder that almost reached Heaven', whereas her murderer – a man she had never met – is 'groveling somewhere below'. And the article framing Mrs Trott's letters reinforces the distraught mother's point of view. Readers of the article would have seen a mother imploring the female friend of a daughter who was 'the essence of refinement' to bring a 'fiend' to justice, thereby contradicting the evidence of the 'fiend's' children.

Remarkably, this exchange between the main witness and the victim's mother, an exchange that should have resulted in a mistrial, seems to have concerned only Mareo's counsel. When her letters and Stark's replies became public, Mareo's solicitor did apply for a commutation of the prisoner's death sentence on the basis '[t]hat the obtaining of the conviction of Mareo became a duty she [Stark] undertook for Mrs Mareo's relatives and a matter of the greatest personal importance to herself'.[29] However, there was never any official response made to these allegations, and it is clear from the article in which the letters were published that *Truth* and presumably most of its readers were not troubled by Mrs Trott's intervention. Nor was there any public outcry about the correspondence between the two women, a correspondence that also included a cable from Stark to Mrs Trott after the first jury had delivered its verdict, and a reply from Mrs Trott thanking Stark for her part in bringing Mareo to justice.

These letters were only published soon after the second trial and so could not have influenced the juries. However, it is clear that Stark's testimony about her friend's refinement and abstemious habits and Mareo's heavy drinking, verbal abuse of his wife and callous refusal to call a doctor accorded with the conventions of Mrs Trott's melodrama. This was also the story told by the Crown, particularly after the first trial, when Meredith decided to make more of Mareo's lesbian accusation. It is likely, therefore, that the two juries, and especially the second, would have shared the same motivations as Mrs Trott – not only to bring 'a fiend to justice', but to clear the name of a virtuous woman. Indeed the logic of the case dictated that a guilty verdict and a verdict that cleared a Pure Woman's name were the same thing. Mrs Trott had observed in one of her letters that 'Deeming (a notorious killer) was a scoundrel; he murdered his wives, but he faced the gallows like a man. He did not drag his wives' names through the mud to save his skin'.[30] Although *Truth* reported after the second trial that Mareo's 'allegation against his wife after she had died by his treacherous hand and he was within the clutches of the law were [sic] also the subject of much comment', it also makes it clear that all this comment had been made during the trials. Thus, while unlike the heroes of melodrama the men of the juries could not actually rescue the heroine from the clutches of the villain, they could rescue her spiritually by restoring her reputation.

The adversarial nature of courtroom proceedings and their culmination in the dramatic dénouement of the verdict mean that criminal trials are particularly amenable to the hyperbolic dichotomies of virtue and vice that characterise melodrama. As in other Western countries, melodrama was probably the most popular dramatic genre of the nineteenth century, but it remained popular in the early twentieth century in film and in the 'new journalism' of papers such as *Truth*, particularly when its subject matter was feminine.[31] However, only a guilty verdict in the Mareo trials would have produced a clear melodrama. While not guilty verdicts can sometimes be represented as melodramatic vindications of the accused's innocence, this could not have been the case here. If the juries had decided that it was not clear 'beyond reasonable doubt' that Mareo had murdered his wife, a moral cloud would still have hung over the musician, if only because his behaviour had been less than exemplary. A not guilty verdict would not have morally vindicated Mareo.

But even to the extent that it could be equated with innocence, a not guilty verdict would have implied, given the logic of the case, four possible basic alternative narratives, all of which are far less compelling than the melodrama we have been describing. A not guilty verdict might imply that, for all their unusual aspects, the Mareos were really just a normal middle-class family which had suffered the tragedy of the accidental death of one of its members. However, this is hardly a satisfying narrative since it leaves death in a contingent realm that lacks any moral dimension. Alternatively, if the death of Thelma was a consequence of the couple's morally flawed or depraved lifestyle, then why should only the wife pay and the husband be allowed to return to his previous life?

Given the historical context of the case, the remaining two narratives are more plausible and yet still far less ideologically compelling than the melodrama about the virtuous woman poisoned by the brilliant but depraved musician. We have been stressing the importance of the discourses of female purity in early twentieth-century New Zealand, but of course there were also counter discourses of equal if not greater ideological power. New Zealand literary nationalism was soon to myth-ologise – or at least subsequently be seen by many to mythologise – the figure of the New Zealand male as a Man Alone battling against a stultifying matriarchy of wowsers.[32] Obviously, however, while all the talk about Thelma and Stark's feminine virtue was very likely to provoke the ire of the country's more conventionally masculine types, a loquacious, overdressed and cosmopolitan musician was hardly a Man Alone figure.

The fourth alternative was that there were misogynist discourses in New Zealand as in other Western countries that might have portrayed Mareo as a battling Breadwinner figure victimised by two evil lesbians. However, this would have been even less convincing since, not only was Mareo as little like a conventional Breadwinner as a Man Alone, but such a narrative would imply, as we have just argued, that sexual perversion could be found within Godzone. A guilty verdict would imply a far more comforting picture of New Zealand society than the four alternatives implied by an acquittal.

The melodrama that emerged from the trials was convincing in part because, as Harcourt argued, it reproduced that oldest of social structures, the sexual triangle. Because of all the positive publicity Mareo received before his arrest, there is no reason to doubt Harcourt's claim that many women did find Mareo an attractive figure; certainly he was much admired by many men. However, for all his charm Mareo was the kind of man who got women into trouble, and the kind of man who could easily be resented by men. Moreover, by turning him into a diabolical wife-poisoner, public opinion was not just warning women against falling for dubious foreign theatricals and cutting down for men a proverbial tall poppy. Mareo's vices – alcoholism, drug abuse, violence against women – were also those of many New Zealanders, including, in all probability, some of the members of the jury. By convicting Mareo, the vices of New Zealand men were in a sense also being denied.

But, as we have been suggesting, there is a more fundamental story underlying this sexual triangle. Not only had Mareo poisoned his virtuous wife with a dangerous and yet medicinal drug, and then befouled her reputation with the allegations of alcoholism and sexual perversion, but he had also introduced an attractive and yet morally dubious bohemian lifestyle into a small country still in economic depression. Mareo the *pharmakon* had killed a virtuous woman with a *pharmakos* and thereby infected the body politic. By pronouncing Mareo guilty, the juries were containing the dangerous aspects of the 'artistic', denying the existence of sexual 'perversion' (or keeping it safely closeted), and re-establishing a clear boundary between New Zealandness and foreignness. The courtroom melodrama in which the male jurors backed by public opinion rescued the reputations of two virtuous women and cast from the body politic a dastardly wife-poisoner was also a tale of the re-establishment of social order. At a time of considerable anxiety about social and sexual purity, the Mareo trials were in one respect a form of social hygiene.

CHAPTER SEVEN

In the Condemned Cell

It is sweet to dance to violins
When Love and Life are fair:
To dance to flutes, to dance to lutes
Is delicate and rare:
But it is not sweet with nimble feet
To dance upon the air!
—Oscar Wilde, *The Ballad of Reading Gaol*, (1896)

IN NEW ZEALAND the institution of what Americans call 'Death Row' can be traced to the 1752 English statute entitled 'An Act for Better Preventing the Horrid Crime of Murder', that specified that 'felons had to be placed immediately after conviction in solitary confinement, where they could do no work and receive no visitors other than the priest, their only solace during the ritual preparation for their death'.[1] Even in 1936 the vestiges of these requirements remained, to the extent that condemned men were not allowed to mix with other prisoners or to engage in any form of prison work, or join in educational or recreational activities, and were guarded around the clock. A light always burned in the Condemned Cell. The mental torture of waiting in the Condemned Cell was acknowledged by judges in Britain at this time, who insisted that executions be carried out as swiftly as possible – on average within six weeks of conviction (even allowing for appeals).[2] Mercifully, the daily weighing ritual, designed to ensure that authorities always knew the necessary length of the 'drop' without letting the prisoner know that the day of execution had actually arrived, did not occur until after a final decision about the condemned man's fate had been made. Nevertheless, it took another sixty years for the Privy Council formally to rule (in the context of a Caribbean legislature where capital punishment still existed) that a lengthy stay in the Condemned Cell constituted 'cruel and unusual punishment', and was therefore unconstitutional. The fact that this judicial recognition of the most serious of constitutional breaches was so long in coming should not diminish the reality of the suffering of any condemned prisoner at any time and in any country during the intervening period. While it is ludicrous to suppose that any such prisoner would, if asked, have opted for death over a life lived under sentence of death, it is perhaps unsurprising that it was reportedly with at least a measure of relief that the torment of waiting was over that many in the end went to the gallows.

Since Mareo was to remain in the Condemned Cell for more than two months, it can safely be assumed that he received his fair share of 'cruel and unusual punishment'. Remarkably, however, he seems to have faced his ordeal with some degree of equanimity, at least eventually. Prison records show that five weeks after receiving his sentence a Catholic priest was permitted to see him. Mareo also saw the prison chaplain, Rev George Edgar Moreton. A former scoutmaster, amateur oarsman, and secretary of the Discharged Prisoners' Aid Society, Moreton was a kind of left-wing muscular Christian and outspoken critic of the punitive aspects of New Zealand's 'hopelessly archaic' prison system. According to him, while Mareo – a courageous, 'gifted, [and] sensitive soul' – was in the Condemned Cell following his second conviction,

> something happened. He spoke to God. When he had first come into that prison he was, not unnaturally, bitter, cynical, resentful; he had deliberately demanded pen and paper in order to sign himself as an atheist. His adored daughter Betty had pleaded with him to say his prayers – he never forgot her words: 'Please, Daddy darling, for my sake, say your prayers'. But her plea had left him unmoved. . . . Lying awake in that dark cell one night shortly after his second conviction he remembered his daughter's pathetic plea and, because he loved her so dearly, he tried to pray. From that moment a wonderful peace came upon him. His mind felt soothed and refreshed, and he knew in his heart there would be no hanging; indeed, so calm did his mind become that he commenced writing his oratorio.[3]

Interestingly, a letter written by Mareo to his lawyer about a week after he had seen the Catholic priest suggests that his frame of mind was by no means inconsistent with this 'conversion' story. It is worth quoting in full because so few of his letters survive and few are as personal:

My dear Mr O'Leary, –
I want to thank you with all my heart for the splendid and noble way you defended me at the trial. That the verdict was an adverse one is no fault of yours: no man could possibly have done more for me than you did. I was enthralled by the brilliant genius of your final address, and, believe me, knowing your generous and sincere nature – when the unexpected verdict was announced – I felt for you and knew that you were suffering.

God bless you for your warm-hearted friendship in my tribulation. It has helped me to maintain an undaunted spirit despite the buffets and jolts which Fate has dealt me.

Strange to relate, notwithstanding everything, my spirit is really undaunted, and I can honestly say that I refuse to allow force of circumstances to break my heart.

It hardly seems credible that after ten months in prison (over two of which I have spent in the condemned cell) I can still find it possible to smile. So I suppose I am entitled to look upon myself as that somewhat rara avis, a 'cheerful loser'. After all, I have a lot to be thankful for, I have found many REAL friends.

I am more than lucky in that God has blessed me with the wonderful love of Betty and Graham (indeed in having their love I am the richest man in the whole world!) and my faith in humanity is restored by the genuine sympathy and kindness shown me by everyone in authority at Mt. Eden Gaol. I cannot speak too highly of their treatment, and my welfare and comfort are studied in every way. Above all, I feel, intuitively, that the many kindnesses I am constantly receiving are prompted by a belief in my innocence, and this has been a great help to me in enabling me to maintain my cheerful and confident demeanour.

And of course, deep down inside me is the knowledge that somehow, at some time in the future, God will readjust matters so that my dear son does not have to go through his life bearing the stigma of his father's tragic misfortune and ignominy.

God bless you, dear friend, I want you to know that my

heart is full of gratitude to you, and that I shall pray for you always.
Sincerely,
Eric Mareo.[4]

Apparently, the indomitable optimism of Mareo that many had commented on before his arrest could survive even two months in the Condemned Cell.

Of the many loyal supporters referred to by Mareo in his letter, Betty was, as Rev Moreton recognised, the most important. According to *Truth*, Betty was allowed to visit her father daily after the first trial, a fact that, in the absence of any other concrete information, became the basis for a feature article. Its author begins by imagining Mareo '[a]lone in the condemned cell, except for the unfailing company of the lynx-eyed warders' and his memories of the 'joyous years . . . writing popular compositions in London; controlling the music for stage shows in Australia and New Zealand; working on plays; winning the melody dear to his strange soul – warped, it is now shown – from the orchestra of his creation'. And then in all his desolation a kind of angel appears – the 'charming Betty Grey, otherwise known as Betty Mareo'. In the account of Betty's visits that follows, *Truth's* portrait of Mareo's daughter is little short of hagiographic. In the space of a single newspaper column Betty is described as 'gracious', 'charming', 'slim', 'attractive and well-dressed', a girl of 'magnificent sympathy and compassion', 'amazingly self-possessed', with 'twinkling footsteps' and a 'gentle voice'. Thus Betty is placed in the same angelic camp as her only slightly older stepmother, rather than in the shameful realm occupied by her father. Although the melodramatic arc of Mareo's life from the 'joyous' London years to the 'ashes' of a 'shameful death' is in a legal and social sense irreversible, the fact that he is still loved by his daughter suggests the possibility of some kind of spiritual redemption.[5] Apparently, a man who has been cast out of society for assaulting a pure woman can be redeemed by the love of another.

However, as the prominence given to the exchange of letters between Thelma's mother and Stark might suggest, most of the women involved in Mareo's life were avenging rather than redeeming angels. For, in the same article about Betty's prison visits, *Truth* reported with some relish that there had already been an abundance of applications from persons wishing to assume the job of Mareo's hangman, and, indeed, that one of the applicants was a woman:

> Once the idol of many women as, immaculate, well-groomed, accomplished and self-possessed, he conducted his Symphony Orchestra, Mareo is tasting the dregs of humiliation and degradation.
>
> For a woman, one of the sex that admired the poise of the polished musician, has applied to the authorities to hang Mareo! It is an application without precedent in New Zealand, and the most devastating blow to his pride that could be imagined. . . .
>
> 'Truth' now reveals how numbers of people have hastened to apply for the grisly task of hanging the musician, among them a member of the sex whose affections Mareo so easily accepted – and spurned. Blind adoration of the majority has been transformed into the merciless, calculating estimate of the condemned man's worth by individuals of the sex.

The article then speculates about this woman's motivation, wondering if she is acting out of economic necessity (how much one wonders could the fee be?), a desire for 'notoriety', or simply by the belief that hanging 'a wife-poisoner, would be a smashing gesture'. After providing a graphic and lingering description of the execution procedure, it concludes by asking whether a woman would be capable of the 'elimination of sentiment' and 'nerve' needed to carry out the 'grim, shocking formalities necessary when the State takes a man's life?'[6]

No official record of such a request, nor of one from any other would-be-hangman, exists. There is one letter on file signed by 'a mother' exhorting the Minister of Justice to '[d]o the right thing' on behalf of the women of New Zealand and 'hang him up at once and save the country from any more expence [*sic*]', but she is appealing to the Minister's 'man hood' rather than applying for the job herself.[7] However, while *Truth*'s story sounds

– from the point of view of a tabloid – too good to be true, it hardly matters whether or not it is. *Truth* did not achieve the highest circulation of any newspaper in the country by featuring stories people did not want to read.

Significantly, the story about vengeful women was perpetuated by those who believed in Mareo's innocence as well as those convinced of his guilt. Harcourt's main contention, as we have seen, was that the men who wanted him hanged were racked by sexual jealousy and that the women were consumed by a desire for revenge. At the time of his arrest, according to Harcourt, '[t]he women of the town, for the most part, were deeply sympathetic and quite sure – that is before the trial – that it was all a ghastly mistake'. However, once the trial got under way, '[t]he Court was packed (mostly with Mareo's former admirers) day after day, and many salaciously minded females reveled in seeing rumours transformed into facts by the authoritative backing of the Crown'.[8] Supporters and detractors alike seemed to believe that there was a kind of sexual triangle in which Mareo initially seduced and then betrayed his female audiences while their men felt, depending on one's point of view, either sexually jealous or protective of their wives' and sweethearts' virtue and honour.

Accordingly, those who appealed to the Crown not to hang Mareo tended to represent the musician in the same kind of way as those who wanted him dead. We have seen how Mareo was frequently represented by those who believed in his guilt as an 'enigmatic' and contradictory figure, but those who begged the Minister to spare his life invariably also drew attention to his unusualness. The woman who felt compelled to inform the Minister that Mareo was 'funny and peculiar' because he did most of the housework (as well as playing the piano late at night), and the correspondent who drew his reader's attention to the connection between the 'super-normal' and the criminal, were both opponents of the death penalty. Similarly, 'a large body of Hawkes Bay citizens', in petitioning the Minister not to hang Mareo, pointed to

[t]he extraordinary conditions prevailing in the domestic life of the Mareo family, the effect of drugs upon the mental state of

Eric Mareo at the time of the death of his wife, and the difficulty of judging him according to the ordinary canons of conduct without prejudice.[9]

Given that one of the election planks of the Labour Party had been the abolition of capital punishment, Mareo might have been heartened by the fact that there had been a change of government in the same year as his arrest. Moreover, since 1900 only a third of those convicted of murder in New Zealand were actually executed. The rate of execution had increased somewhat in the fifteen years before his arrest to exactly half of the twenty-six men sentenced to hang, but it was still low enough, presumably, for Mareo and his supporters to fancy his chances. No doubt as a direct result of the verdict in his first trial, the press's interest in the new Government's stance on the death penalty surged during February and March 1936.[10] Questioned on the subject by the *Weekly News,* the Minister of Justice stated that '[o]ne plank in the platform [of the Labour Party] is "Abolition of capital punishment and flogging". That is a fact. It always has been a plank. All members of the Labour Party are bound by it'.[11] Nevertheless, when in April a member of the parliamentary opposition, W.J. Broadfoot, asked in the House whether the Government intended to legislate to abolish the death penalty on the current session, he was advised merely that 'the matter . . . is receiving attention'.[12] The resulting uncertainty was reflected in an article appearing on 19 June 1936 in the *Hawkes Bay Herald* – occasioned no doubt by Mareo's conviction for the second time two days earlier. Under the heading 'Will Labour Allow the Death Penalty?', the *Herald* reported that '[t]he attitude taken by the present Labour Government is subject to much conjecture', and quoted the Speaker of the House, W.E. Barnard, as saying:

> A good many years ago, the Labour Party decided that it was opposed to capital punishment . . . that decision has never been reversed but it is also true to say that the question has probably not been raised in anything like a definite form for many years.[13]

Four days later *Truth* reported that the 'feeling is strong against granting a reprieve to Mareo' amongst both the Labour members and 'the rank and file of Parliament'. The source for this information was presumably the Labour member for Auckland East, F.W. Schramm, who, while

> personally opposed to capital punishment . . . could not find a thing to say in favour of this poisoner. Mareo had been declared guilty by two juries and five judges of the Supreme Court, and that left no doubt of his guilt. . . .
>
> Discussing his answer afterwards, Mr Schramm admitted that it would be fairly typical of the views of the Labor members of Parliament. There was no sympathy, it was said, for a man who, when granted a second trial, used it to call evidence to blacken the name of a woman – his wife – whose tongue was stilled.
>
> From the point of view of an opponent of capital punishment, he continued, it was unfortunate that such a case was the first that would have to be decided by the new Labor Government.[14]

Ultimately, the fate of a person sentenced to death was decided by the Executive Council who were bound to consider the judge's view, petitions and letters from friends and, where the condemned man's sanity was at issue, the reports of the appropriate experts.[15] Accordingly, a week after sentencing Mareo to death, Mr Justice Callan had written in confidence to the Attorney-General enclosing the notes of evidence, the case on appeal (which included the exhibits), and a transcript of his summing up. Most significantly, the judge expressed to the Attorney-General his personal reservations about the outcome of the trial. He said that while Stark struck him as a reliable witness,

> . . . the expert medical testimony called for the Prosecution did not satisfy me that it necessarily follows from the symptoms observed and recounted by Freda Stark, that Mrs Mareo must have had a further dose of Veronal in the milk, or at about the time the milk was given. So far as I could follow the matter, that was not shown to be better than a probable opinion.[16]

His Honour went on to record that his doubts were only increased by the medical evidence tendered by the Defence. He concluded:

> [I]t thus follows that I could not finally convince myself of Mareo's guilt except by consideration of the other evidence. But consideration of these other matters, even collectively . . . has not had the effect of carrying my mind beyond grave suspicion. I can get no certain help from consideration of possible motives. Mareo failed badly as to sending for a doctor. He told lies, and his conduct before and after his wife's death suggests strongly he was nervous about something, and was hiding something. But I am not satisfied that his nervousness was not about the medicine bought from Morgan.[17]

At about the same time, the Attorney-General received a lengthy formal representation from Mareo's solicitor, K.C. Aekins, who formally applied for a commutation of Mareo's sentence on eight separate grounds, the principal of which – apart from jury prejudice – involved the unreliability, irrelevance and inconsistency of the Crown's medical evidence. Interestingly, he also pointed out that, while Mareo had been incapable of forming the necessary intent to murder because of the influence of the veronal, the Defence had been unable to pursue and develop a plea of manslaughter because of their client's express instructions. Presumably, as a man innocent of murder, Mareo would only have been satisfied with an acquittal. The Attorney-General, Mason, also formally sought and received the views of Counsel for the Crown, Meredith, and for the Defence, O'Leary, as to the possibility of Mareo's innocence. O'Leary's reply (no doubt in the knowledge of the lengthy representations which had been made by Aekins) was brief. He simply said:

> . . . I wish to state that from the very first time I saw Mareo he protested his innocence of the charge brought against him, and this attitude he has maintained to me and to his solicitor throughout.[18]

In contrast, Meredith expressed complete satisfaction with the jury's verdict despite finishing his report with the somewhat contradictory admission that 'taking Mareo's condition prior to his wife's death into consideration if the jury had found a verdict of manslaughter instead of murder I would not have considered that an improper verdict'.[19]

Betty and Graham Mareo also wrote both to the Governor-General and to Mason. In the letter to the Attorney-General, Betty based her plea for clemency on the apparent bias of the second jury, saying:

> I am afraid I know very little about legal matters, my only experience being the trial and retrial, which recently took place in the Supreme Court at Auckland, but I do not understand how it is humanly possible for a jury to decide on a verdict in such a short space of time – less than an hour and a half – when a brilliant man like Judge Callan gives four and a half hours to sum up the case after due consideration of the facts, it seems to me an amazing thing and utterly beyond my comprehension; perhaps I do not understand justice.
>
> We believe Daddy to be innocent and beg your consideration of our request.[20]

In fact, it was to the Under-Secretary for Justice, Berkeley Lionel Scudmore Dallard, that the job fell of considering all the correspondence and the Judge's report, and of making a preliminary recommendation to the Minister. Dallard, who was also Controller-General of Prisons, was a former accountant who had been Under-Secretary since 1925 and was widely regarded as an efficient, but rigid, unenlightened and conservative, man. Personally, he supported the retention of both flogging and the death penalty, but not because he believed that they were effective as deterrents. Rather, Dallard simply felt that such punishment was necessary to 'satisfy the claims of justice'. An extract from a memorandum written by Dallard in 1931 to the superintendent of the Wellington prison regarding the procedure for executions perhaps gives a further indication of his character:

[A]s the Union Jack is emblematical of British justice, such a flag will be hoisted to the main flagstaff on the morning of the execution. At the time the execution takes place a black flag will be hoisted to the lower flagstaff, the Union Jack in the ascendant, silently proclaiming the suzerainty of the law.[21]

All in all, then, it might be thought that Mareo was unfortunate in having Dallard as the man who would, in the first instance at least, make a judgement about whether he should live or die. Indeed, in his memorandum to Mason, Dallard makes it quite clear what his recommendation would usually have been in such a case:

[P]oison murders involve deliberation and callousness, and for a vindication of the law and the satisfying of the public conscience, in ordinary circumstances, the extreme penalty of the law should be given effect to . . .[22]

Happily for Mareo, however, it is apparent that Dallard placed great store in the reservations expressed by Mr Justice Callan in his report. Moreover, the apparent inconsistency in the approach of the two juries was not lost on the Under-Secretary. '[G]iven the influence of drugs at the time of the alleged offence,' Dallard wrote, the first jury's recommendation of mercy was probably justified, but '[t]he absence of such a recommendation by the second jury suggests an unconscious bias against the accused with a possible predisposition to discount the later medical evidence submitted by the defence.'[23] On 24 July, Mason circulated this memorandum and the other relevant documents to his Cabinet colleagues.[24] According to *Truth*, when Mareo

was visited in the Condemned Cell by a senior warder and told of his fate, he turned eagerly towards the grim messenger who stepped into the cell.

'Your sentence has been commuted to life imprisonment.' The words struck Mareo like a blow. His shoulders slumped. Life seemed to ebb from him. Then he squared himself, turned and marched with the warder from the cell.[25]

CHAPTER EIGHT

'J'Accuse': Facts and Phalluses

THE MAREO TRIALS HELD a mirror up to New Zealand society that reflected, at least initially, a less than comforting image. And after the commutation of the sentence certain individuals, aided by the bureaucratic machine, went to some lengths to ensure that Mareo remained in gaol. However, the tale of professional and bureaucratic inertia, tunnel vision and, on occasion, downright dishonesty that this bespeaks should be balanced by another tale. From the very beginning Mareo had his supporters. Some were musicians who had worked with him, but many had never met the man. Most simply recognised that a terrible injustice had been committed and, even during the war years when the world was preoccupied with rather more important matters, they were quite tenacious in their various campaigns for his release. If Mareo's years in gaol show the lengths to which people will go to defend prejudice, they also show the extraordinary persistence of reason in the face of prejudice. Although the trials and their aftermath reflect an image of a rather repressive and conformist society, they also reflect the fact that the country could support a not inconsiderable number of men and women committed to speaking out against injustice.

This is not to say that all of Mareo's supporters were entirely reasonable. Mrs Irene Holmes, for example, wrote to the Minister of Justice to inform him that at a meeting of their 'neighborhood circle' in the 'chapel' a '"visitor" came through, as the expression is, and began in a faltering whisper' to communicate a message relevant to Mareo's fate. Apparently neither Mrs Holmes nor the 'visitor' were aware that Mareo's life was no longer in danger, because the latter, who identified himself as the notorious murderer Bayley, having departed this world a few years earlier and 'been through hell', declared that he was now 'alright', repentant and, not surprisingly, an opponent of capital punishment.[1]

Others were reasonable but just eccentric. One such was a Dr G.M. Smith, a Scottish immigrant to the 'backblocks' of Northland. Dr Smith had read about the first trial in the newspapers and realised, on the basis of his extensive experience with a babiturate (nembutal) similar to veronal, that the Crown's doctors' 'principle' that a patient could not relapse into a coma was wrong. Initially Dr Smith contacted Mareo's counsel, then wrote to the Minister of Justice (assuring him that the Prime Minister could vouch for his seriousness), and later acted as a medical adviser for the Defence during the second trial. However, as the Department of Health discovered when it made enquiries about his professional standing, Dr Smith had 'his own ideas about dress' (including the assumption that a doctor could wear his hair long and shirts without ties and shamelessly unbuttoned), and was generally known as 'an advocate of lost causes'.[2] The Whangarei police were later to elaborate on Dr Smith's dress sense, noting that

> he either goes bare-footed in-doors or in Hospital, or only wears sandals outdoors. He always wears a canoe shirt, wide open at the neck and chest, sports jacket and grey slacks. He appears in the Supreme Court witness box in this garb, but his eccentricity in dress is probably envied by Bench and Counsel, especially in summer weather.[3]

And on the subject of Smith's outspokenness, a close acquaintance, Sir Douglas Robb, would later write – rather grandly – that Dr Smith was

> . . . a unique character, one of great natural endowments, but tortured inwardly, who was ready to tilt a lance at established pomp and humbugs. One thinks of Ajax defying the lightning, of Ulysses deriding Polyphemus, or of Don Quixote charging the windmills – all done in the guise, almost the garb, of an Old Testament prophet. Dr Kemble Welch [Smith's biographer] thinks of Socrates, the self-styled gadfly, stinging society

into a greater awareness of its collective crimes, follies and misfortunes.[4]

It may well have been Dr Smith's flamboyance that made Mareo's lawyers refrain from calling him as a witness. However, he remained a tireless campaigner for Mareo's release, detailing the flaws in the medical aspects of the Prosecution's case in a book of medical reminiscences written after the trials.[5] Interestingly, the author of the Whangarei police report, Detective Sergeant J.B. Finlay, plainly admired Dr Smith's medical abilities, crediting him with being 'one of the first, if not the first doctor, in New Zealand to fully appreciate the value of suphalilamide [sic] drugs' and concluding that '[p]ersonally, I have a rather high regard for Doctor Smith and consider that I could best describe him as a "rough diamond" but no fool'.[6] Despite such advice, Dallard, the Controller-General of Prisons, was dismissive, writing in a memorandum to the Minister of Justice that 'it is fairly common comment that Dr. Smith of Rawene is somewhat of a crank'.[7]

But the vast majority of Mareo's supporters were not so colourful. In October of 1940, E.G. Hemmerde KC, the Recorder for Liverpool and one of Britain's most distinguished criminal lawyers, read the reports of both trials at his sister's request (who presumably knew, or knew of, Mareo when he lived in England) and concluded that 'there is a grave danger that here has been a serious miscarriage of justice', largely on the grounds that, since there is no reason to suspect that Whitington and the Rianos were not telling the truth, it was 'quite incredible' that Stark was speaking honestly 'when she said she never knew Mrs Mareo to take drugs'.[8]

However, the most important opinion came from the man on whose medical opinions, ironically, the Crown's case had largely rested, Sir William Willcox. At the instigation of Mareo's 'friends', Sir William read a full transcript of the first trial and 'some information about the second trial', formed the view that Stark's evidence was unreliable, and concluded that it was '*not . . . at all likely that a third dose was given* on Saturday night' [original emphasis], and that a 'self-administered' dose on the Saturday morning had caused her to die of 'Veronal Pneumonia'.[9] Subsequently, two petitions were submitted to Parliament calling for a review of the case primarily on the basis of this report. On 30 November and 1 December 1942 Parliament's Statutes Revision Committee met to hear the petitions. Both Crown prosecutors attended the hearing as did O'Leary, together with Mareo's solicitors, K.C. Aekins and Hugh Roland Biss.

In the words of Sergeant Hamilton (who was in attendance and took notes) Mareo's supporters 'divided their attack'. First, Biss told the Committee that statements made by Stark to the police were in material respects at odds with the evidence she had given at trial. Biss contended that when these earlier statements were compared with Stark's testimony, it became apparent that her evidence had been 'developed' to fit the Crown theory of the case. He argued that because the Defence were not shown the earlier statements they had been denied the opportunity to put the discrepancies to Stark and, therefore, the opportunity potentially to undermine the 'sheet anchor' of the Prosecution.

These allegations were the cause of some controversy in the Committee, not because it was thought that in withholding the statements the police were guilty of any wrongdoing, but because it was evident that Mareo's lawyers had seen the police files containing Stark's statements *after* the trials. Biss told the Committee that the files had been made available by the Minister of Justice, Mason. Mason, who was present at the hearing, took full responsibility for the matter, and is recorded as saying 'that if it came to the point where the file could not be available and truth and Justice were going to suffer he would get out of it', by which he presumably meant he would quit politics.

O'Leary then dealt with the Willcox Report and went through Whitington's evidence of Thelma's pre-existing veronal habit, saying that he was a truthful witness. O'Leary also read aloud the three 'lesbian' letters, although his object in doing so is unclear from Hamilton's report.

From the Sergeant's notes it appears that the principal

preoccupation of the members of the Committee, in common with all Mareo's detractors, was his 'failure' to take the witness stand. O'Leary simply responded that he took full responsibility for that decision, saying it was made on the best judgement he could exercise, including his concern that, were Mareo called upon to testify, matters peripheral to those at issue would be unduly emphasised to his detriment. To emphasise the point, O'Leary referred to the fact that it appeared that Whitington's credibility as a witness had been unfairly damaged in the eyes of the public (and the jury) merely because he admitted to being separated from his wife.[10] On 4 December the Select Committee recommended that no action be taken on the petitions.

Undeterred, Mareo's supporters decided to petition the Prisons Board in the following year not once but twice, largely on the basis that the Statutes Revision Committee 'being composed of lay-men were not in a position to properly value and appreciate the medical aspects of the case'.[11] Both petitions were unsuccessful. In the same year a third petition was made to Parliament and was heard by the Statutes Revision Committee. Unsurprisingly, given that its membership was identical, this Committee was no more sympathetic than the first. Of these petitioners, perhaps the most noteworthy was Captain Harold Montague Rushworth. Educated at Oxford and a former engineer for the London Flying Corps, officer in the Royal Flying Corps during the Great War, farmer in the Bay of Islands, and a Country Party MP for ten years allied with the Labour Party, Rushworth has been described as 'the cinema ideal of an English gentleman'.[12]

The following year, 1944, what should have been a crucial submission was made by Sir William's successor as the Senior Official Analyst to the British Home Office, Dr Roche Lynch (who had, incidentally, been offered, but declined, the job of testing Winston Churchill's cigars for poison). Dr Roche Lynch concluded that Thelma had died of pneumonia as a consequence, in the first instance, of having self-administered veronal on the Friday night, and, in the second, of having taken a further dose, probably in 'an automatic state', on the Saturday morning.

However, perhaps the most telling aspect of this report is its comments about the Crown's medical witnesses:

> I recognise that Dr. Gilmour and the other doctors, and also the analyst who gave evidence at both trials on behalf of the Prosecution, gave their honest views throughout but it is equally clear that they were labouring under a considerable disadvantage in that they had only experienced a very few cases of veronal poisoning, and were quite unfamiliar with certain aspects of such cases. . . . The New Zealand medical witnesses do not appear to have realised that a person who has taken a possible fatal dose of veronal can become completely comatose and subsequently regain more or less complete consciousness, and then relapse into a coma without taking any further doses of the drug. . . . The conclusion reached by the New Zealand doctors that Mrs Mareo must have taken a third dose of veronal on the Saturday night for the reason that she regained consciousness and later again became comatose is based on inadequate knowledge of the effects of this drug.[13]

This report was the basis for a third petition to Parliament that was heard in October 1944. Meredith again appeared, but this time Mareo's supporters were represented by Arthur Sexton. Meredith submitted reports from Mr Griffen and Drs Gilmour, Lynch and Ludbrook in rebuttal of the report by Dr Roche Lynch, and Sexton not unreasonably sought an adjournment so that he could consider, and seek expert advice on them. The adjournment was rather grudgingly granted but the hearing was never reconvened. It seems the petition was overtaken by the events of 1945 and was eventually formally withdrawn in 1946.[14]

The apparent ease with which the relevant authorities were able to dispatch these petitions might suggest that Mareo had no supporters within the realms of officialdom, but this was not the case. As we have seen, no less a personage than the Minister of Justice and Attorney-General, H.G.R. Mason, had an interest in the case that verged almost on obsession. His archive at the National Library contains hundreds of pages relating to the trial, including the first few pages of a book he was writing about the case when he died in 1975. These pages exist in perhaps a dozen only marginally different versions, as though his book were mirroring its subject matter – his endless and unsuccessful attempts to prove Mareo's innocence.

Mason was a reformer and a man widely regarded, during a parliamentary career that stretched from the first Labour Government of 1935 to his enforced retirement in 1966, as the conscience of his party. Furthermore, as a practising theosophist, vegetarian and teetotaller, he probably understood better than most the pressures within New Zealand society towards conformity. However, Mason was also a lawyer and a mathematician and therefore someone trained to pay attention to the minutiae of a case irrespective of his moral convictions. Thus the most original aspect of his case for the release of Mareo was his close attention to discrepancies between Stark's early statements to the police and her testimony during the trials. In part, these concerned the degree of Thelma's alleged period of consciousness before she received the milk. For example, whereas Stark claimed during the trials that Thelma awoke of her own accord just prior to receiving the cup of milk, in one of her statements to the police she said that she could not keep her awake even though she 'shook' and 'nudge[d]' her. They also concerned the time of this period of alleged consciousness. Again, according to Stark's testimony at the trials, Thelma's request to go to the lavatory was made while Mareo was out of the room preparing the milk, whereas in one of her statements to the police she said that '[i]t would be fully an hour and a half from the time that she mentioned that she wanted to go to the lavatory that we took her there', which must have been some time before she received the milk.[15] In short, Mason demonstrates that not only does Stark's later testimony increase Thelma's degree of animation or consciousness, but it also transfers her period of greatest animation from the beginning of the evening to a period just before she was given the milk.

In addition to the discrepancies noted by Mason, a comparison of Stark's statements to police and her evidence reveals other potentially significant omissions and points of departure. In particular, a reduction in emphasis on the amount of alcohol consumed by Thelma is apparent. While in a long statement made two days after Thelma's death, Stark denied that Thelma drank to excess, she said 'Mrs. Mareo was a moderate drinker and was fond of liquor' and said that she would drink a bottle of brandy a week, but that she also drank wine. She admitted that Thelma had been 'under the influence of liquor' at the party on the last night of *The Duchess of Danzig* and recounted how Thelma had told Dr Walton that she had been drinking and that he had told her 'that it would benefit her health if she did not drink as it was no good for the nervous state she was in'. Thelma then told Stark that she was going to give up alcohol. Stark recorded two occasions on which she had taken wine to Thelma at home and that on the first she (Stark) 'opened a bottle at about 3 pm as the deceased wanted a drink'.[16]

By way of contrast, in evidence at the second trial all Stark said on the subject was that Thelma *might* have been 'under the influence' at the *Duchess* party, that '[w]hen I did see her take a drink, she would generally drink sherry, probably a full wineglassful', and that on the night of the Dixieland party 'Thelma and I were alright that night as far as sobriety goes. We had had a little wine'. Stark flatly denied the Rianos' allegations about the amount of alcohol Thelma had consumed on certain other occasions.[17]

A similar reduction in emphasis can also be seen if the statements made by Freda Evans to the police are compared with her testimony at the trials. For example on 24 May 1935, Evans said to the police that

[o]n a number of occasions at the house I saw her take sherry . . . Mareo told me on one occasion when I called that his wife was in bed and . . . I asked him what was the trouble with his wife and he told me that it was her failing that she took drink. I saw her in bed and he begged her to take a cup of coffee which she reluctantly accepted and when she sat up I noticed in my opinion that he was under the influence of liquor. She had her senses but it was noticeable to me that she had been taking liquor.[18]

After Mareo's arrest in September, Evans made a further statement to the police about the incident, in which she seemed to suggest that Mareo offered Thelma drugs rather than coffee, and that Thelma 'was pleased to accept'. She then records Thelma as saying to Mareo, 'You're fond of drugs too aren't you?'[19]

Nothing about this incident made it into Mrs Evans's testimony at trial. Rather, she simply said:

> I did not at any time during rehearsals or during the performances see Mrs Mareo under the influence of liquor. . . . I have been in their house on several occasions . . . I never saw her under the influence of liquor in her own home. The only time I ever saw her take anything was a glass of sherry . . . On one occasion Mareo told me his wife drank too much.[20]

We can only speculate that it was no accident that several of the statements made by people regarded at an early stage by police as potential witnesses, but later not called by the Prosecution, also spoke of Thelma being a 'heavy drinker' or as having 'a strong smell of liquor' during rehearsals for *The Duchess*. Given the amount of evidence called that emphasised the opposite (effectively that Thelma 'never' drank), it cannot be assumed that the Prosecution simply regarded these statements as irrelevant.

More tantalising as far as the subject of Stark's pre-trial statements to the police were concerned was the omission of any reference in her later evidence to her allegation that she herself had been the object of Mareo's unwelcome attentions. On 17 April 1935, she recounted to the police what had happened after Thelma's funeral that morning. According to her statement, she and Mareo were in the sitting room at Tenterden Avenue when

> Mareo told me 'You know I was in love with a small person but I did the right thing by Thelma and made myself forget about it.' He was referring to his affection he had for me . . . Mareo had made love to me before he married Thelma but I resented his attentions and he had cooled off . . .

Stark went on to say that Mareo's advances resumed after they had met again in Auckland and that he had told her in that context that Thelma wouldn't mind as 'she has been a wife to me only in name'. She continued that after the funeral

> [h]e said 'I know that Thelma was in love with you because she told me.' I understood from that that Mareo meant his wife had been a lesbian. He also said other things which I do not like mentioning which include [words omitted from statement] . . . he said 'Of course I was very considerate towards her and I very rarely bothered her and when I did I never finished inside her.' He said consequently this made me a nervous wreck and I suppose you have heard of such a thing as wet dreams and I used to have them and I was ruined physically.[21]

It makes sense that the Crown would not have wanted Stark to repeat these statements about Thelma's sexuality in the court-room. But why did the Crown not question her about Mareo's alleged attempted seduction when clearly this would have counted against him? The only answer we can venture is that talk of Mareo's sexual attraction for her might have endangered her perceived objectivity or neutrality towards him. It might, for example, have allowed Mareo's counsel to imply that she was either prejudiced against Mareo or, somewhat less plausibly, that she might have even welcomed his sexual attention.

It appears, then, that there was some truth in the allegations made to the Select Committee that Stark's evidence changed after her interviews with the police so as to better suit the Crown's case. Nor do the changes appear to have been limited to the issue of whether the fatal dose must have been in the milk. These changes were quite subtle and it is possible, given the kinds of pressure to which she was subjected and the period of time that elapsed between her first interview with the police and the second trial, they were made quite unconsciously.

For Mason, however, the issue was more fundamental. He formed the view that Stark's statements to the police were less than honest. A memorandum he wrote to Cabinet in 1945 – which finishes by recommending the establishment of a Royal

Commission to inquire into Mareo's case – outlines what he believed to be her motivation and is worth quoting at length:

[t]he case has its origin in a story told to detectives by Freda Stark of Mareo's refusal of her repeated pleas to him to get a doctor. And this story cast its shadow over every scene of the resulting drama . . . The files leave little mystery. The story is only to save herself from sharing the blame for the delay. It is not merely the odium (such as later befell Mareo's secretary [Brownlee]) of not understanding the urgency of medical attention. She learnt from Dr. Dreadon [the doctor called to the house] that trouble was impending for the delay, and when she met detectives she had her story ready, setting herself and Mareo poles apart and exalting herself at Mareo's expense. She and Mareo had been unanimous in thinking at first there was no urgency, because they supposed the illness to be the normal result of abortifacient medicine, and especially because six months earlier Mrs Mareo had gone through at least one experience exactly similar in all respects, real, and supposed, except for the fatal ending. They were also unanimous (when alarm at length arose) in their efforts to avoid a criminal charge against the patient. This caused further delay. Of the two, she was much the more averse to getting a doctor. She alone caused the final and fatal delay of the last 24 hours. While Mareo was sleeping on Sunday afternoon she observed in the patient a new and terrible symptom of the sort which next day heralded imminent death. She concealed this from Mareo. She had indeed food for thought in Dr. Dreadon's words! And little wonder she fainted in [the Lower] Court upon the relaxation of the tension when she safely got through the ordeal of her first public recital of her exculpatory story![22]

Given that Mason campaigned for many years for homosexual law reform, it is unlikely that these accusations were motivated by any kind of homophobia. And they are also quite plausible. Since Mareo had been arrested on the flimsiest of evidence, Stark would perhaps have had good reason to fear prosecution. Nevertheless, it should be added in her defence that she was a young and inexperienced woman no doubt in a state of shock as a consequence of her lover's death. Furthermore, as a 'lesbian' she had, unlike Mareo, good reason to fear the prejudice of the police, the judiciary and her 'peers'. And, of course, she was not to know that her perfectly understandable denial of any kind of 'lesbian' relationship was going to rebound on Mareo. If Stark's probity was not of the highest order, the homophobia of the day was certainly a strongly mitigating circumstance.

Soon after the matter was considered and rejected by Cabinet, Harcourt published his defence of Mareo under the pseudonynm of 'Criticus', possibly because he feared some kind of official action against him. Significantly, the book was called *I Appeal*, its title presumably alluding to 'J'Accuse', Emile Zola's famous open letter protesting the imprisonment of the Jewish Captain Alfred Dreyfus on the notorious Devil's Island. Harcourt would later emigrate to New York where he would become the rector of an Episcopalian church in Long Island and an educational reformer. The biographical note to one of his books published during this period describes him as 'probably the only Anglican clergyman of this century whose pen has been largely responsible for an important legal reform: the estab-lishment of a Criminal Appeal Court in his own country'. Although it is unlikely that *I Appeal* was 'largely responsible' for this reform, it did, nevertheless, provoke quite a reaction.

I Appeal is partly an imaginative re-enactment of the Mareo trials and partly a condemnation of the repressive aspects of New Zealand society. In addition to the courtroom drama, this rather odd book also included a strange fiction in the form of a cautionary tale about how an imaginary 'model village' or 'the pride of democracy' can win the battle against fascism but only by adopting the methods of its enemy. Whereas the Labour government 'might have been reasonably expected to offer some resistance' to various authoritarian tendencies, Harcourt argues, under wartime conditions '[m]any thoughtful students of modern political trends have not failed to observe a disturbing similarity between National Socialism in Germany and the Labour Govern-ment's version of socialism in New Zealand'.[23] Although the comparison of the Labour Government with Nazi Germany is rather forced, to say the least, there had indeed been severe curtailments of civil liberties during the war years. Pacifists, conscientious objectors, Communists, foreign 'aliens', Jehovah's Witnesses and others were jailed on various charges usually amounting to alleged 'subversion', and freedom of expression was severely curtailed. According to the historian Nancy M. Taylor,

> [t]he paradox appeared that in New Zealand, where the [Labour] government's background might have led to considerate handling of conscientious objectors, those who would not fight received much harsher treatment than did those in Britain and other Commonwealth countries.[24]

Both Harcourt's specific and general claims could not, perhaps, be lightly shrugged off.

But Harcourt's general allegations and some of the more specific ones put by Mason were not to be answered by a Royal Commission. Instead, he got his wish for a Court of Criminal Appeal when the Criminal Appeal Act 1945 was passed in December. In the last major step that remained open to Mareo's supporters, an appeal was duly lodged and heard in March and April 1946.

The principal grounds for the appeal were orthodox enough and they are discussed together with the Court's response to them in more detail in the chapter that follows. However, there was one far more bizarre matter that was raised by Mareo's lawyers in chambers and that has never, as far as we are aware, been made public.

On 15 April 1946, 11 years to the day after Thelma's death, it appears that Mareo's lawyer, Arthur Sexton, sought to introduce further new evidence in support of Mareo's acquittal. He had in his possession a signed declaration by George Scott Russell, which said,

> In 1936 I was the Associate to Mr Justice Callan during the hearing of the second trial in *Rex* v *Mareo*. I was on the floor

of the Court looking at the exhibits lying on the court table. One of the plain-clothes Police officials (I am unable at this date to state who this official was), in the course of conversation with those around the table, including myself, pulled out a phallus from his pocket and jokingly said this was the kind of thing they had been using. . . .

The phallus I saw on the above occasion was a dark rubber penis-shaped article, which the Police official producing it said had originally come from France. There was a slit in the end of the phallus and the Police official said the phallus contained Vaseline in its sac which, on contact with the body, trickled out. I cannot now remember whether the official who produced the phallus was in any way connected with the case.[25]

In seeking to introduce this evidence at the hearing of the appeal, presumably Sexton wanted to show that the police had suppressed evidence that they thought would harm the Prosecution's case. Sexton's thinking must have been that if such a phallus had indeed been found by them on the Mareo premises, and produced at the trial, the jury would have been confronted with undeniable, tangible evidence that Thelma and Stark were 'perverts'. In the words of Inspector S.G. Hall of the Auckland police, 'Mr Sexton brought the matter of a phallus before the Judges in Chambers with the view of damaging Freda Stark's evidence.'[26]

Not surprisingly, the story of the phallus produced an immediate and somewhat frantic reaction within the Police Department. An extensive internal inquiry took place but, again unsurprisingly perhaps, yielded no clue as to the existence of the phallus or the identity of the police official in question.

Other than to remark on the general oddity of this turn of events, there is probably little that can be concluded from it. Since it seems most unlikely that Russell made the incident up, it is possible that the police did find a 'phallus' at the house and chose to suppress this evidence. However, it is far more likely that a police officer produced a phallus that he had acquired by other means simply as a 'joke' with his fellows. In either case it does perhaps reinforce what we have argued above about the kind of damage that might well have been done to the case against Mareo if Thelma and Freda had been openly acknowledged as lesbians. In the end, however, it made no difference to Mareo's appeal. According to the Commissioner of Police: 'the Judges ruled out the evidence of the phallus as being inadmissible.'[27]

CHAPTER NINE

A 'Topper' in Mt Eden Gaol

NOT SURPRISINGLY, the unofficial campaign against Mareo was spearheaded by *Truth*. A few months after the commutation of his death sentence, to one of life imprisonment with hard labour, the paper reported that Mareo had been 'Making Money While in Gaol' since music composed by him (including a foxtrot improbably entitled 'Prison Patrol') had – according to an unnamed 'London Newspaper' – been 'smuggled' out of prison. The other prisoners – who think him a 'topper' and who 'are very sore about . . . his snobbishness' – thought that he was making the money for his son.[1] A few years later in 1940, the paper also published an article with the heading

GLAMOUR BOY OF TOUGHEST GAOL:
CONVICTS JEALOUS OF ERIC MAREO
HIS AMAZING PRIVILEGES

According to this article, these 'privileges' were: 'a "cushy" job in charge of the prison library, with a large room and a fire'; an extra pair of socks every week; permission to have his lights on later at night; 'frequent use of the prison piano'; and permission to wear a watch.[2] Perhaps in a New Zealand prison during the 1940s these really were 'amazing'; certainly as far as *Truth* is concerned they indicate that the mere fact of his imprisonment has not significantly altered Mareo's 'glamour' status. Although Auckland society of the Depression years had been replaced by the routine of Mt Eden Gaol, a cigarrette holder and black tie by a wristwatch, nothing has otherwise changed in Mareo's relationship to 'ordinary' New Zealanders.

Needless to say, *Truth*'s account of the 'cushy' life of the Mt Eden 'glamour boy' was somewhat at variance from reality. Mareo had been granted some of these 'amazing privileges' (prison records do not mention the extra pair of socks), but they were in recognition of his 'excellent service' in directing the prison choir.[3] The royalties were from music published before his imprisonment and were used to pay off previous publishers' advances. Crucially, however, the tabloid failed to mention aspects of Mareo's personal life, about some of which, given the diligence of its investigations, it must have known. Five months after the second trial, Mareo's father, Raimund Pechotsch, wrote to the Controller-General of Prisons, Dallard, asking him

> to please get my son to write to his mother who, through this, is in a Hospital in Sydney and is almost demented with her terrible grief.
> If she could see a letter from her son in his own handwriting perhaps her grief might be lessened. The state of my wife's mind is so terrible that, in spite of all we can tell her to the contrary, she has formed the impression that he has been hung.[4]

As well she might, in view of her age and the fact that her son had been twice in the Condemned Cell. Mareo did write to his parents, but, as his father informed Dallard less than a month later, '[u]nfortunately his reply came too late [since] his [mother] died on the 23rd of Dec and she was too ill to read it'.[5]

If *Truth* knew about the death of Mareo's mother (which is not unlikely), it was not mentioned in the first of its articles about Mt Eden's 'glamour boy', and in the second no reference was made of the fact that on 8 May 1939 his beloved daughter, Betty, died after an operation in England. According to Moreton, the prison chaplain, when he broke the news,

> [t]he wretchedness of the fifteen minutes in which I spoke to the broken-hearted Mareo will never be forgotten. With tears running down his cheeks he told me about Betty, how she had asked him to pray; he told me of her sweetness, her courage through all the dreadful ordeal, he told me how both he and Graham . . . had adored Betty; how much she meant to them both. The last words I heard as he left the private room in which we had had the interview were: 'Poor, darling Betty. Poor Graham. God give me strength.'[6]

Two years later Mareo's father died (of cirrhosis of the liver and soon after having remarried), and then Graham was killed in France, apparently a few weeks after receiving the Military Cross for his part in the Normandy invasion. A lieutenant at the time, Graham was shot by an unknown person while off duty and wandering the streets of a French town. None of these tragedies was mentioned by *Truth* when it began its campaign a little more than two years later to prevent Mareo from being granted parole.

In the same year as Graham's death, 1944, the Auckland criminal and divorce lawyer Richard Singer published a book entitled *24 Notable Trials*. The book was based on an earlier series of radio broadcasts by him and included a chapter on the Mareo trials; 'the first time', he claimed, 'that the case [had] been presented to the public in detail'. Although Singer does give a reasonably accurate account of the known facts, albeit with some rather slanted editorial comments, he barely deals with what he acknowledges was the 'most important' medical evidence 'around which much contest raged', preferring to resort to a panegryric about the New Zealand juryman who would always, he claims, 'do his duty conscientiously, fearlessly, and justly'. Strangely, for a criminal defence lawyer (at least by today's standards), Singer then makes the usual criticism of Mareo for not taking the stand and of his counsel for daring to rely on the fact that the onus was on the Prosecution to prove its case. Moreover, he goes on to make the astonishing suggestion that

the jury may well have said to themselves that they were quite able to dismiss from their minds all points of mere prejudice which might be brought up against the accused from a perhaps not too palatable past career, but that there was one other thing that they were also capable of, and that was that they were able to judge an innocent man when they saw him, and particularly when they heard him, if only by the very manner in which he declared his innocence.[7]

In other words, the mere way in which Mareo uttered the phrase 'not guilty, your Honour' might have been enough to justify his conviction.

There can be little doubt that the publication of Singer's book and the prior broadcasting of its contents would have been influential both in terms of the general public and of those more closely concerned with Mareo's case. And while it is less likely that *Truth* had much influence over the officials responsible for Mareo's fate, it did reflect the waves of public opinion to which the ears of some politicians were keenly attuned. Accordingly, the members of the Parliamentary Statues Revision Committee that met on three separate occasions over a period of approximately two years to consider the pleas of Mareo's various petitioners may well have been less than open-minded about the evidence placed before them. Certainly, the chair of the first Committee, F.W. Schramm, had already made up his mind, since, as we have seen, he was on public record, as having 'not . . . a thing to say in favour of this poisoner' and being in 'no doubt of his guilt'. Nonetheless it should be noted that when the Committee reported its verdict to Parliament on 4 December 1942, F.W. Doidge, a former journalist and member of the opposition National Party, did speak in Mareo's favour. (Once described by his former employer, the newspaper magnate Lord Beaverbrook as 'The Man who got the Million' [readers], Doidge also wrote an eight-page letter to Mason the following year that was subsequently published in at least one newspaper. In this letter Doidge pointed out that the 'atmosphere' of the trials resembled the 'hysteria' he had witnessed at two recent murder trials in London involving husbands accused of poisoning their wives.[8]) However, the members of the Committee who spoke after Doidge fiercely contested his claims, and at least one, the Member for Remuera, William Endean, seriously clouded the issues with what would now be called 'misinformation'. According to him, Betty was the only witness to give evidence that Thelma was 'addicted to drink', Thelma 'must have been given almost the whole contents' of the cup of milk, Mareo had initially denied possessing veronal, 100 grains of veronal were found in Thelma's stomach, and Sir William Willcox was a 'paid advocate' for Mareo.[9] According to Endean and two of his fellow Committee members, these facts showed that, since it was impossible for Thelma to have acquired any veronal on the Saturday morning, the lethal dose must have been administered in the milk on the Saturday night. As Endean said, 'it would have been a miracle' if an ill woman 'who was only 5 ft. 2 in. in height' could have reached the 'dress-basket' [*sic*] in the wash-house where the empty veronal bottle was found.[10] Apparently, Endean was unaware that Detective Meiklejohn had testified that '[i]f a person had something to stand on, any normal person could get a bottle out of that suitcase',[11] that even the Crown's medical witnesses had thought it possible that Thelma had taken veronal on the Saturday morning, and that Graham had mentioned finding his stepmother apparently searching for something in her dressing table that morning. As for the Willcox Report, the speakers dismissed its conclusions on the grounds that Sir William had not been present at the trials, and Endean even claimed that '[t]he whole of his statement is full of bias, and his evidence of the woman being an addict to drugs and drink indicated that'.[12]

The other main grounds for the petition, the inconsistencies in Stark's statements and evidence, did not seem to trouble any of the speakers, only Endean bothering to deal with some of the less important ones, and then only so that he could assert that 'those facts did not go to the root of her evidence and did not affect her credibility'. As Endean then proceeded to tell the House,

> [t]he fact remains that for two trials under severe, grueling cross-examination, that woman stood out, and the jury believed her. There is one thing that emerges out of this strange, weird, and peculiar household, and that is that Miss Freda Stark behaved like a woman. [*Time extended.*] She was most solicitous for this unfortunate woman. I am not going into the details of the woman's death, because they were very harrowing. I did not consider the sentimental side, but purely the legal aspect.[13]

Somewhat later, when another member enquired about Mareo's motive, Endean returned to the issue of 'this strange, weird, and peculiar household':

> I do not want to go into that. There are sordid features, but we are not concerned with that aspect of the matter . . . It would not be reasonable for us to rake up the terrible details of that household and the unhappiness of the family.
> Mr HOLLAND. – I was not aware of that aspect of the case.
> Mr Endean. – I do not think that the Committee members allowed those considerations to enter into their minds, when they were coming to a decision.
> Mr BODKIN. – The evidence proved that Mrs Mareo was a good woman.
> Mr Endean. – Yes.[14]

Not surprisingly, the second Committee that met the next year spent considerably less time than the first considering the pleas of its petitioners. After the hearing was over, Mareo's lawyer, A.G.T. Sexton, made the following revealing comments about its proceedings to one of its dissenting members, Cyril Harker:

> Dear Harker,
> Our hearing finished up in the usual unsatisfactory way that hearings have before Select Committees in that we only had half the members present in the afternoon that were present in the morning. Whether or not it would have made any difference of course is more than doubtful.
>   I must say that although I expected strong opposition I was dumbfounded at the state of mind of most of the members. Their minds seemed to me to be quite closed and it was impossible to get them to see any important difference between the statements which Freda Stark made to the police and her evidence at the trials. . . . Richards of course has got it 'in the back of his head' that Mareo gave his wife veronal at some time, never mind the evidence . . . [15]

When the Committee again reported to Parliament, Mason spoke at length against its recommendation, but the National

MP, Walter J. Broadfoot, objected to the amount of time the House had already wasted on the petitions and concluded by stating that '[a] great deal too much sympathy is being expressed for Mareo, and much too little is being expressed for the murdered woman. I think the women of the country feel that justice has been done'.[16] The only other speaker was the Prime Minister, Peter Fraser, and he also complained

> that I think the bringing of this case before the House session after session has become altogether too attenuated. We cannot get a better jury, or a fairer body of men, than the Statutes Revision Committee. . . . We should see justice done not only to the living, but, also, we should not forget the tortures of the lady who died, and the torture of the other lady, who had to undergo such a terrible experience and grueling time in the witness-box . . .[17]

Like courtrooms, parliamentary debating chambers are also excellent venues for melodrama.

In fairness to the politicians, however, there had been considerable work done to discredit the petitioners and their evidence even before it reached the Statutes Revision Committee. Some of the medical experts, for example, were subject to personal and professional investigations that seemed to amount to *ad hominem* attacks. We have seen how Dallard let his view be known that Dr Smith was 'somewhat of a crank', but in none of his memoranda about him does he mention that he was in many respects a remarkable man whose medical credentials, at least, were unimpeachable. In the same memorandum, Dallard also tells Mason that the Prisons Board (which also considered the Willcox Report several months before the first Statutes Revision Committee) had

> [c]ome to the conclusion that Sir William Willcox's report was, to say the least, presumptuous and could only have been made by a man who was failing mentally. By a strange coincidence of events, almost following the Board meeting I received a copy of an English journal 'The Medico-Legal and Criminological

review' which had an obituary article written by Dr. Roche-Lynch, an eminent Pathologist in England [who would, of course, conclude the following year that Mareo was innocent], and he, whilst paying tribute to the great work that Sir William Willcox had done, quite frankly states that Sir William Willcox had failed considerably mentally in the evening of his days – the report on Mareo, as you will recall, was written within a week or two of his death and was not actually signed by him.[18]

Mason underlined the second use of the word 'mentally' and wrote in the margins '[n]o, a misinterpretation', as indeed it was: the obituary simply stated that '[d]uring the last eighteen months of his life he did not enjoy the best of health, and latterly it was clear that he was failing', a statement which clearly refers to his *physical* health.[19] In fact, Sir William's report is entirely lucid. Presumably, then, Dallard told the Board about the obituary or at least his deliberately misleading interpretation of it before the Board considered Sir William's report. Indeed, Dallard's bizarre phrase 'almost following' seems like an unwilling confession that the obituary may not have been received *after* the Board meeting.

But the substance of Sir William's and Dr Roche Lynch's reports were also attacked. At varying times their reports were sent to the doctors who had given evidence for the Crown and the Government Analyst involved in the case as well as to a New Zealand pathologist called Dr Philip Lynch (not to be confused with Dr Roche Lynch), who found that the verdict of the jury 'was a justifiable one'.[20] Clearly, the reports of these overseas experts were enormously embarrassing to them. For, not only had the former confirmed the Defence's alternative account of Thelma's poisoning, but they had also cast serious doubts on their professional competence. And in this particular instance, the doctors may have been especially sensitive to criticism because they were well aware both that their evidence had always been regarded by the Crown as crucial and that their lack of experience was regarded as being the major potential weakness in the Prosecution's case.

The Crown Prosecutor's concerns in this respect first became evident when, prior to his departure overseas with the All Blacks in late July 1935 and following a meeting with Drs Gilmour and Gunson, he advised the police that he considered the medical evidence was insufficiently strong to justify charging Mareo and that it should be tested first in the less stringent forum of the inquest (which had been adjourned in April and not resumed). It appears, however, that the police were unwilling to pursue Meredith's recommended course because they believed that Betty and Graham 'would not be so reticent' if Mareo were arrested and that 'were the inquest taken first, Mareo would have influence over the two children and they may not disclose all they know'.[21] Accordingly in August they met with the doctors and a Professor Sydney A. Smith, the Dean of the Faculty of Medicine of the University of Edinburgh, who was visiting New Zealand at the time. Although Professor Smith was unwilling to give evidence himself (not wanting to be 'hung up on the case') he felt able to confirm the views of the local doctors. As a consequence of this advice Meredith's partner, Vincent Hubble, recommended to the police that Mareo be charged with murder.[22]

Perhaps the vehemence with which the doctors would later defend themselves is not surprising. Nevertheless, the rhetoric of the New Zealand Dr Lynch's final report verged on the violent. At one point, the overseas expert, Dr Roche Lynch, 'insults the intelligence of his readers'; and, at another, one of his sentences 'is an absurdity'; but in general he defensively concludes that

> I cannot help remarking that I think the observations made by Dr. Roche Lynch in this paragraph [cited above] are both ungracious and discourteous to doctors about whom he can know very little. This attempt to belittle the professional standing of the medical men concerned warrants a close examination and scrutiny of his own statements.[23]

In fact, as we have seen, Dr Roche Lynch had merely written with some degree of understated accuracy that the local doctors had given 'their honest views throughout but ... were labouring under a considerable disadvantage' given their lack of experience with the drug. Since the local doctors had more or less admitted this in court (which was presumably why they relied so heavily on one of Sir William's written reports), it is hard to know how Dr Roche Lynch could have been any less 'ungracious and discourteous'.

However, there can be little doubt that even Dr Roche Lynch's grace and courtesy deserted him when he was shown copies of the reports written by the New Zealand doctors in response to his own. In a further declaration prepared for the purposes of Mareo's appeal in 1945, Dr Roche Lynch begins by thoroughly demolishing the doctors' 'extremely loose' and 'wholly inaccurate' summary of the evidence at the trials and then does the same to their scientific analysis. He concludes

> [i]f the evidence of Sir William Willcox and the evidence contained in my previous Declaration and in this present Declaration had been made available at Mareo's trials, it is fantastic to suppose that any jury could properly have concluded that the prosecution had discharged its onus of excluding all reasonable doubt as to Mareo's guilt. In my opinion Mareo was entirely innocent . . . The matter in regard to the Mareo case upon which no doubt can conceivably exist is that the conviction of Mareo in the light of the evidence now available to the New Zealand authorities could never have been properly resolved upon by the juries. . . . I am quite convinced that there was no veronal in the milk, and that there is no scientific reason whatever to suppose the contrary.[24]

In addition to the impediments presented by the obduracy of the New Zealand medical 'experts', Mareo's petitioners also faced other legal obstructions. About a month before the first meeting of the Statutes Revision Committee, Mason asked Meredith to give his views to the Committee on certain matters such as the alleged discrepancies in Stark's evidence. Soon afterwards, Dallard wrote to Meredith warning him that it 'would be unfortunate . . . for the Committee to gather any idea that keenness to secure a conviction prompted the withholding of any matter that should have been placed before the jury' and that 'both your prestige and that of Mr Johnston . . . may be the subject of comment'.[25] Mason then complained to Dallard that his 'letter too strongly turns the issue into one of an accusation of impropriety of the trial',[26] and after the Statutes Revision Committee had met he wrote to Dallard that 'I am rather relieved to note that Mr Meredith does not consider that his conduct was on trial'.[27]

The reality was, however, that both Meredith and Johnstone had reputations to protect and, in light of the nature of some of the evidence that was kept back by the Prosecution, Mason's question was potentially difficult for them. They certainly did not respond to Mason's request, and it was partly for that reason that Mason later queried Meredith's fee for his services to the Committee of £98 (which the latter then reduced to £75).[28] In August the following year, Mason complained in Parliament that he had still not received a reply from Meredith about the discrepancies,[29] and a year after that he observed to the Solicitor-General that

> Meredith, who should be detached, is really the one in whom I have long been compelled to recognise there is little detachment in this case – he has been quite incapable of considering for a moment any point contrary to the story he has presented.[30]

Significantly, the Mareo case is not even mentioned in Meredith's 1966 autobiography *A Long Brief.* This is remarkable given the prominence of the trials and the fact that Meredith discusses at some length several other cases involving veronal poisoning while saying, quite erroneously given his successful prosecution of Mareo, that no one had ever been convicted of committing murder with veronal.

As we have seen, the person mediating in many cases between Mason and all these various parties was Dallard, who, as well as being the Controller-General of Prisons, was also Mason's Under-Secretary at the Department of Justice. Shortly after his contretemps with his Minister about his warning to Meredith, Dallard wrote to Dr Philip Lynch, venturing the opinion that 'it may be that the Jury concluded from the whole surrounding circumstances of the case that Mareo had been pushing veronal into his wife with every meal since the Friday morning, or since she started taking a glass of milk before going to bed'.[31] In a subsequent memo to Dallard, Mason objected to his 'inventing and cluttering up the case with new and unfounded suggestions', and demanded that he 'cease this process of invention'.[32] Dallard replied, indignantly, that while he was 'in the unhappy position of not being *ad idem* with you', 'any Permanent Head who shapes his opinions to conform with what he believes will please the Minister, besides being dishonest, is no real help in the long run'. Of course Mason was demanding no such thing. Even more extraordinary, however, was Dallard's claim that he was entitled to his opinion because '[t]he *truth* in this case is known only to Mareo, and no other human being can ever reduce the problem of Mrs Mareo's death to the realm of ascertainable fact', a claim which if true could only have justified a not guilty verdict.[33]

As the Controller-General of Prisons, Dallard also sat on the Prisons Board. When Mareo made his first address to the Board in November 1944, he claimed that its Chairman had previously told him not to make any further submissions because 'outsiders' were making efforts on his behalf.[34] According to Rev Moreton in Harcourt's biography, Mareo

[t]old me that the authorities had forbidden him to mention the case – or his hopes in connection with his release – in any letters to relatives or friends. *They had informed Mareo that nothing whatsoever would be done for him. When Mareo had mentioned the names of Sir William Willcox and Mr E.G. Hemmerde the authorities brushed them aside as so much nonsense.* [Original emphasis.][35]

Although Mareo's claim that he had been forbidden to make any case to the Board was 'immediately challenged',[36] it seems unlikely that he was lying. For what other reason would he have delayed making submission?

Mareo also petitioned the Board a few months later in April 1945, three days after he had heard the news of Graham's death. There were two aspects to his plea, one concerning the 'punishment-value' of his sentence (in which he writes movingly about the impossibility of exaggerating 'the actual horror of going *back* into the Condemned Cell to await what appeared to be an inevitable hanging'[37]) and the other concerning his desire to return to England to help Graham's widow with the education of his two grandsons. Unfortunately, however, Graham's distraught widow had just written to Mareo saying that she had discovered soon after his death that Graham had been having a 'lengthy affair' with another woman and that as a consequence she wanted to cut all ties with Mareo.[38] The Superintendent of the prison sent the letter to Dallard with the curt comment that the aspect of Mareo's plea relating to his desire to return to England so as to earn money for the education of his grandsons 'does not now seem necessary'.[39] Accordingly, Dallard wrote to the Superintendent of Mt Eden (as he was to do on many subsequent occasions) asking him to inform Mareo that his petition had been denied.

There was one further bizarre aspect to Dallard's involvement in Mareo's case. Following the publication of *I Appeal*, he made inquiries about the identity of its author, and then wrote what amounted to a long review of the book, which he signed 'Rhadamanthus' (who in classical mythology was the son of Zeus and one of the judges of the Underworld). The review was sent to various officials and to Schramm, the chair of the Statutes Revision Committee, with the following explanation:

[A]lthough I consider the book a poisonous publication calculated to shake public confidence in the administration of justice . . . I do not propose to issue the attached review for general publication for the reason that Mareo has served nearly ten years' imprisonment, and it might not be fair to him at this state to publish anything that might prejudice his rehabilitation when released. . . . You understand the review is not an official statement but simply expresses the view of what may be regarded as the ordinary man in the street who in the ordinary way comprises the jury. I hold strongly to the view that a jury of honest men of ordinary intelligence is just as competent to arrive at a conclusion on facts as are learned Judges or experts.[40]

Just a few weeks earlier, the Solicitor-General had written to Mason expressing the conviction that there should be an 'elaborate reinvestigation' of all matters surrounding the case, particularly Mason's suggestion that the police had not made available the files containing Stark's initial statements.[41] Perhaps Dallard had been driven into the thankless job of book reviewer because he feared that there would be the Royal Commission recommended by Mason. As it turned out, however, a Royal Commission was deemed unnecessary with the passage in December of the Criminal Appeal Act of 1945, which con-ferred greater powers on the Court of Appeal in criminal proceedings (for which Harcourt would modestly claim credit), and Mareo's counsel successfully applied for leave to appeal. This was perhaps bad luck for Mareo because, according to legal authority (as cited by Dallard), if an appeal court comes to 'the conclusion that there was sufficient evidence upon which the jury could have arrived at their decision, they are bound to uphold the conviction, even if they entertain a doubt, for it is the jury alone who are judges of fact'.[42] By contrast, a Royal Commission is bound only by its terms of reference and within them is free to form its own (admittedly non-binding) conclusions on the matter under inquiry.

Mareo's lawyers based their appeal on three grounds. Firstly, they claimed that fresh medical evidence not available at the trials refuted the medical evidence of the Crown. However, since the Willcox and Roche Lynch reports were matters of opinion rather than fact, the Court rejected this claim. Secondly, counsel argued that Stark's testimony at the second trial contradicted both her testimony at the first trial and her earlier statements to police. This was also dismissed, the Court holding that Stark's evidence was not 'diametrically opposed to, or seriously in conflict with, her previous statements'. As a consequence, the fact that Stark's statements to the police had not been made available to the Defence did not 'call for careful and serious consideration'.[43]

But it was the four judges' conclusion about the third ground of the appeal – that the conviction at the second trial was unreasonable and could not be supported with regard to the evidence – which seems most unconvincing. The Court stated that this ground rested upon two 'fallacies' 'which seem to have continued ever since in the minds of the prisoner's supporters'. The first of these concerned the imputed claim by the Defence counsel that '[t]his is murder or nothing', which the judges quite rightly dismissed because the possibility of a manslaughter verdict had in fact been put to the second jury.[44] However, the second of these 'fallacies' was

> [t]hat the charge against the prisoner stood or fell solely on the question whether it was proved that there was veronal in the milk which the prisoner gave his wife early on the Sunday morning. It is true that the theory of the Crown was that the ultimate and lethal dose of veronal had been administered through that medium; and, if the guilt of the prisoner depended upon the correctness of that theory being proved, the question whether a verdict of guilty was satisfactory or not would require consideration. But in truth the prisoner's guilt did not by any means depend solely upon whether the death of the deceased was caused by a dose of veronal administered in the milk on the occasion spoken of. The suggestion that the final dose of veronal was administered on that occasion was no more than a theory advanced by the Crown.[45]

There had certainly been some confusing discussion of this issue in the Court of Appeal, since Meredith informed the judges that the Crown's case had been that 'veronal was given on the Friday night, Saturday morning, and in the afternoon, and a mass of other circumstances'. In fact, in his closing address to the jury at the second trial Meredith had said

> [T]he whole point is this: How did Mrs Mareo get that dose? If you find that she got it in that cup of milk, then that must mean that Mareo gave it to her. If you have any doubt about it, any reasonable doubt about it, then it is your duty to give Mareo the benefit of the doubt. But if your consideration forces you to the conclusion that the veronal was in the milk, I would ask you to give a verdict in accordance with your finding.[46]

Clearly, Meredith was telling the jury to acquit if they thought the fatal dose might have been administered in anything other than the milk. Thus his portrayal of the Crown's case to the Court of Appeal was nothing short of misleading. The appellate judges were also no doubt confused by the statement by Mareo's counsel (neither of whom had participated in the trials) that '[t]he Crown says he gave her a *lethal* dose . . . on the Friday night' [our emphasis], which the Crown certainly did *not* say at either of the trials since they simply claimed that he had administered a non-lethal dose on that occasion.[47]

Nevertheless, it is hard to understand how the judges could have believed that the Crown's contention that the lethal dose was in the milk was '[n]o more than a theory'. The Crown's case (or even 'theory') was that Thelma would *not* have died from any of the doses of veronal taken before the Saturday night. That was the whole point of their contention and the vast bulk of the 'expert' medical evidence that a person who had come out of a veronal-induced coma could not then relapse. The Crown's proposition that the fatal dose was in the milk was not 'a theory' or even 'the theory' but their entire case. Indeed, the judges virtually concede this with their claim that '[t]he theory of the medical witnesses for the Crown . . . was treated at the trial and has been treated in this Court as having an undue importance'.[48] But even if it had been given 'undue importance', on what other grounds could the jury have 'reasonably' concluded that Mareo murdered Thelma? There was no other 'theory' or possibility put to them. It was not even open to the Crown to claim that Thelma had died of a dose administered on the Saturday morning, since its own medical 'experts' seem to have conceded that Thelma may have taken a dose then of her volition. In doubting the validity of the Crown's theory of the case, the Court of Appeal was logically also doubting the safety of the jury's verdict. Yet the verdict was nonetheless upheld.

CHAPTER TEN

Golden Years

AS A CONSEQUENCE of the Court of Appeal's decision, all avenues of relief were now effectively closed for Mareo. It was simply a matter of how long he would remain in prison. This did not, however, reassure Mrs Trott. In October 1946 Messrs Watney Sibun & Sons, Funeral Directors of Newmarket, applied, at her instigation, to have Thelma's decade-old remains disinterred and cremated in New Zealand. Mrs Trott's reasons for this request were explained in a letter to Dallard:

> [F]irstly we have no one there to look after the grave. Secondly the fear of that man expressing the wish to be buried there. It would be too terrible for words after taking nine months to take her beautiful young life [?] . . . I am nearing the journey's end almost 82 and will meet my beloved child in a better world than this.[1]

Dallard had already written to her advising against this action on the grounds that it would provoke 'further publicity'.[2] In his reply to this letter he decided not to grant Mrs Trott's request, and she replied thanking him for 'your advice and kind expressions' and resolving to 'try and console my self with the thought my little girl is better off'.[3]

However, others had expressed concerns that if Mareo were released from prison he might commit further crimes in this world rather than the next. About a year after Mrs Trott's sad request, the Prisons Board had indeed recommended that Mareo be released on probation in May of the following year, 1948. No reasons for this recommendation were given but it was by no means unusual: by that time Mareo would have been a 'model prisoner' for more than twelve years, or about two years more than the average sentence served by murderers at the time. *Truth* somehow got wind of this recommendation and on 1 October 1947 questioned how the Prisons Board could have decided that a man who murdered with poison was 'no longer a danger to society' when, by contrast to the murderers who act 'in the heat of violent passion or on the impulse of the moment',

> [t]he poisoner works with calculated cunning, doing his victim to death in the most cold-blooded manner, exerting every wile to assure that his crime goes undetected. Diabolical cruelty is the essence of the nature of the person who slays by poison.

Mareo not only deserved a longer sentence than other murders; he also needed to be kept in prison because a poisoner 'is more likely to repeat his crime than any other type of killer'.[4]

Six days later, the issue was raised in Parliament. Broadfoot asked Mason whether there was a specified time a person convicted of a capital offence must serve. Mason replied that the Prisons Board decided the matter of releases for prisoners, not the Minister of Justice. Another National MP, Ronald M. Algie, asked the Minister 'when convicted murderers, after having been softly and gently cared for in the prisons, would be let loose ["to have another go" according to newspaper reportage] upon a suffering public?' Broadfoot then pursued his original question, insinuating that '[t]he persistence of the efforts on [Mareo's] behalf suggested that some sinister influences had been at work, and that the Prisons Board was releasing the prisoner as a result.' Mason's objection to the expression 'sinister influences' was upheld, and he then made the rather surprising admission that when he received recommendations for the release of prisoners he sometimes glanced through them, sometimes not, and that on this occasion he had merely 'notice[d]' the name of Mareo. Predictably, another National MP, Hilda Ross, replied that this 'would not reassure the public, especially women'.[5]

Nor did it reassure *Truth*. Commenting on this typically scurrilous exchange in the House, the tabloid protested that

> [i]t would be a travesty of justice if all the rejections of the most strenuous efforts made to disprove Mareo's guilt were to

be thwarted by the failure of a Minister to face the facts and realise the seriousness of turning loose on the community a man convicted of the most satanic crime in the criminal calendar.[6]

Broadsheets such as the *Evening Post* and the *Daily Telegraph* also questioned, albeit in less alliterative terms, Mason's casual treatment of Mareo's case, demanded clarification of the term 'life sentence', and, in the case of the latter, reiterated Mrs Ross's concern for New Zealand womenfolk. Again, the demonic qualities of Mareo the outsider were contrasted to the sanctity of the country's women. A world war and more than a decade had passed since Mareo's first conviction, but apparently nothing had changed.

Thus, when Mareo was eventually released in May 1948, *Truth*'s coverage was almost identical to its coverage of the trials. (In a smaller article it also made the bizarre suggestion that Mareo's crime bore comparison with that of Lionel Terry, a man '[s]till alive and in good health in a mental institution' after forty-three years for shooting 'an old Chinese in Wellington on the night of September 24, 1905, as a means of impressing on the public the menace of what he described as the "Yellow Peril"'.[7]) There is the same stress on Mareo's 'well-dressed appearance', except that the ostentatiously held cigarette holder has been replaced by a 'twirling' of his gloves. His 'debonair manner' is the same except that it now contrasts with a postwar society of ration cards rather than a pre-war world of unemployment queues. Mareo is still a 'good musician' and still the 'showman' with 'the air of an artist who had just given of his talents to the less fortunate, or an impresario come to negotiate the showing of a superfilm [*sic*], or arrange a tour for some world-famous musician'. Whereas once his past had been mysterious, it is now his 'future intentions' which are a 'close-knit secret'. He has also somehow managed to acquire £500, a sum suspiciously like Thelma's wasted savings.

But above all there is Mareo's 'jaunty smile'. True, the smile is framed by a 'soft felt hat set at a jaunty angle'; its owner in the two photographs is staring straight at the camera, and it reveals a set of sparkling new dentures. However, it never occurs to *Truth* that the extraordinary smile might be a consequence of its owner's jubilation at being set free after twelve years. Instead, the smile conceals 'any inward sorrow' or 'pricks' of 'conscience' and 'masks the dreadful record of the wearer' as, in one of the photos, its owner 'reclines in the car' that 'whisks' him 'back into society'.[8] Like the smile of Lewis Carroll's Cheshire cat, Mareo's takes on an unsettling life of its own. The smile is fundamentally deceptive and therefore exemplary of its owner's elusive or ambiguous qualities.

Truth did not need to wait long to see what Mareo was up to. A few weeks later he was married again, also in Wellington. Revealing that he had changed his last name to Curtis, thereby deliberately ruining his desire for anonymity, *Truth* also reveals that his bride was Gladys Ethel Andreae, Mareo's physiotherapist in Mt Eden Gaol. Like Thelma, Gladys Andreae is also 'a woman of wide sympathies and considerable artistic taste', but her reputed fortune – 'a third interest in an estate of just under £40,000 left by her father, Charles Oscar Andreae, wool exporter and kauri gum merchant, who died in 1929, and the major portion of the estate left by her mother, which was sworn for probate at just under £7,000', the paper informs us in unnecessary detail – is considerably larger than Thelma's. Not surprisingly, then, the marriage 'came as a shock to socialites in Remuera, as it will to the general public', the implication being that Mareo had targeted yet another innocent woman for her money. And adding to the general air of suspicion is the fact that the minister who performed the marriage ceremony, Rev Jack Broxholme Rushworth, one of 'Mareo's helpers and protectors' and the son of the previous petitioner on his behalf, Captain H.M. Rushworth, had not only complained about the paper's coverage of Mareo's release but had also mysteriously changed from talking frankly to the paper about his friend's innocence to refusing comment as the result of '"legal" advice'. *Truth* denies creating a 'wrong impression' and reiterates the fact, which 'cannot be escaped', that 'Mareo is a free man, apparently in good health and capable of a wide enjoyment of life, who is at the same time a convicted wife-poisoner', without spelling out the obvious implication.[9]

But perhaps there really was some cause for concern. A month after his marriage Dallard wrote to Mareo's Probationer Officer asking why Mareo had not reported to the District Probation Officer while 'holidaying' in Wellington. '[I]t would be unfortunate,' he writes, 'were the public, through the press, to get the impression that our system is a farce and that a probationer . . . can move about the Dominion and live in the district of another Probation Officer without the latter's knowledge and without any form of direct supervision.' Dallard finishes with the alarming question, 'Where is Mareo at present?'[10] By then Mareo had slipped back to Auckland, his 'holiday' unsupervised because his probation officer felt that he 'been subjected to unnecessary publicity which could almost amount to persecution' and had done his 'best to make him feel that we, in this Office, are his friends and not his persecutors'.[11] Nevertheless, Mareo's new friend confessed that his probationer had failed to inform him of his marriage.

Although Mareo's third marriage seems to have been happier than his previous ones, it was unable to revive his failing health. After only a year of married life he suffered what his doctor described as a 'severe coronary thrombosis on 24-4-49'. According to the doctor

> [t]his condition is liable to recur and to be gravely affected by emotional states. He has the very high-powered and dynamic emotional set up which is sometimes found in musicians and he cannot help reacting much more powerfully than the average man to emotional upsets. His having to report [to his probation officer] once a fortnight for a further twelve months is beginning to upset him quite seriously and is likely to affect his heart. I therefore strongly urge that if possible he be now excused all further routine visits to the police.[12]

Mareo applied to Dallard to have this requirement lifted, pointing out that

[t]he fact remains that the necessity of reporting is so very much on my mind that even when I am at work composing, orchestrating or practicing the piano I simply cannot forget it.

I know you will understand when I say that in some indescribable way it is as if I were mentally still in prison.[13]

Although not unsympathetic, Dallard replied that he could not grant this request because it might 'focus further attention on you', and advised him 'if only as an exercise in self-discipline, to face the position stoically for a while longer'.[14] Fortunately, however, Mareo's stoicism was barely tested because two days later the Prisons Board, following representations from Mason, granted his request.

Soon afterwards the Curtises said goodbye to Remuera and its 'shock[ed]' 'socialites' and moved to Ardmore, a small town on the outskirts of Auckland near Papakura, where they purchased, according to Mareo, 'a delightful house built on our section of three quarters of an acre, in very lovely surroundings with a view of both harbours'.[15] They seem to have led a quiet and unremarkable life in Ardmore, even though Mareo did not at first make a very favourable impression on Papakura's probation officer. The latter was of the opinion that he

is a wily individual who is using a subterfuge in order to make his term of probation as easy as possible for himself. I found it necessary to make him report personally on one occasion when I first came here so that I would at least know him.[16]

Seven months later, however, the officer reported that '[h]e appears to be of strictly sober habits and no adverse comment can be passed on his general mode of life'.[17] Four years later, the same officer even reported that being on probation 'seems to have a psychological effect on him and it would seem that he is in constant fear that if he commits the slightest breach of the law his license [for probation] will be cancelled.'[18] Inevitably, prejudice against Mareo always dissipated with familiarity.

As Eric Curtis he did, however, attract some publicity. On 8 August 1951, the oratorio Mareo had begun to write after being removed from the Condemned Cell and following his religious conversion, *The Christ*, was performed for the first time in Auckland by the seventy-strong Ardmore Teachers' Training College choir and a professional orchestra of thirty players. The oratorio received favourable reviews, the *Herald* reporting that '[a]n audience which completely filled the hall heard "The Christ" in a movingly sincere performance that was alive with musical interest' and the *Auckland Star* grandly comparing 'its grace and spontaneous outpouring and . . . its harmonies [to] . . . Donizetti . . . the younger Verdi, and . . . Mendelssohn'.[19] However, two years later Arthur Jacobs, a visiting English music critic of some stature, but notorious for his abrasive manner and negative reviews, heard the oratorio rehearsed by the Christchurch Harmonic Society and mockingly confessed,

> [h]ow choralists who have recently given Bach's Mass in B Minor can devote time to this unspeakable drivel is beyond me.
>
> The presence of the Biblical text must have numbed their critical faculty. Remove the words, play this music in a restaurant, and it would be recognised as an inadequate accompaniment for drinking what in New Zealand passes for coffee.
>
> I really feel that if I can persuade this society to drop this oratorio before it is too late I shall not have come to New Zealand in vain. The thought of healthy men and women spending time on this type of combination of bad Mendelssohn, bad Gounod, bad Saint-Saens, and bad Stainer, when they could be engaged in some relatively uplifting occupation like dominoes, stirs me to a quite personal indignation.[20]

As Jacobs' gratuitous (though no doubt true) comments about New Zealand coffee might suggest, his main intention seems to have been to insult his readers. He begins the first of his five columns: '"Why are you going to New Zealand?" they said in Sydney. "You'll find it's provincial." Of course it is! Any ass can see that.' And he then reports as evidence of this 'provinciality' the fact that the Italian words for 'Ladies' and 'Gentlemen' had been misspelled on the doors at the flying-boat base in Wellington at which he had disembarked.[21] As for other New Zealand composers, Jacobs finds that their 'idiom . . . indicate[s] an isolation which might become dangerous', and more specifically that Douglas Lilburn's Preludes for Piano are 'unfinished and scrappy, calling for correction'.[22] It is difficult to know, therefore, whether Jacobs's assessment can be trusted. Certainly, many of the *Listener*'s readers did not think so, judging by the number of indignant letters protesting his review published in the following two weeks. Nevertheless, perhaps because of Jacobs's influence, when it received its first public performance the Christchurch *Press*'s reviewer found the oratorio 'a thoroughly bad work'.[23] Perhaps because of these reviews, neither Mareo's expectation of the 'strong likelihood' of the oratorio being performed by the BBC choir and orchestra, nor his belief that the National Orchestra would perform one of his piano concertos, was satisfied. Apparently, a Baptist choir in the United States did perform the oratorio during Christmas of 1957.[24] But apart from these performances, and despite the existence of the scores of nearly ninety of his compositions in the British Library, to the best of our knowledge his music has never since been performed. Many of Mareo's compositions were for children and some were popular pieces with mawkish titles such as 'The Dying Rose: A Lament' and 'Crushed Petals'. Nevertheless, the New Zealand conductor and composer, Ashley Heenan, told us that his 'middle of the road' compositions were certainly quite 'competent' and in the second or third rank by international standards. As for *The Christ*, Heenan thought that it had

> a certain curiosity value. It is obviously written by a composer who has lost touch with any contemporaneous influences in his art. It is as though he has experienced a 'time warp' as there is not one sign of the musical developments that took place during the period of his confinement. It is as if all had stood still since his conviction in February 1936.

Just prior to the first performance of *The Christ*, Mareo had written to the Prisons Board informing them of the impending performance and pleading to be discharged from probation. His plea was rejected, although when it was made again the following year the Board did waive the requirement that he report in person to his probation officer. However, Mareo kept applying unsuccessfully every year, explaining in his 1955 application that

> [t]he fact of being on probation is always a source of mental anxiety. One would need to be inordinately phlegmatic not to feel anxious and mentally oppressed as the years pass and one is still what for want of a better description, one can only call 'under open arrest'. With the thought of being 'On probation' as a sort of sword of Damocles over one's head at all times.[25]

Since even his initially hostile probation officer at Papakura had referred to his 'constant fear' that he might unintentionally breach the conditions of his probation, Mareo was probably not exaggerating his 'mental anxiety'. Two years later, his new probation officer confirmed his predecessor's impression that 'Curtis lives a life of fear', pointing out that

> [h]e is scared of publicity and afraid of being involved in a traffic accident. Some months ago Curtis happened to bump into another car in Papakura while parking. He went to the Police Station and, according to the Sergeant, was very nervous over the episode. It was the Sergeant's impression at that time, and still is, that no useful purpose could be served by keeping him on Probation. . . . I believe that Mrs Curtis has, in the past, exercised rather a strict supervision over her husband. This, I am told, is being relaxed now but it has served the purpose of tiding him over what must have been a difficult period of re-adjustment. If there is strain in the home, or if Curtis is not living the life he ought to, it is kept a remarkably close secret.[26]

As a consequence of such submissions, the Parole Board finally recommended on 21 October 1957 that Mareo be discharged from probation in May 1958, assuming presumably that there would be no obstruction from the Minister of Justice. However, since the National Party now formed the government, the Minister of Justice was not Mason but Jack Marshall. In rejecting the Board's recommendation, Marshall, who was a supporter of capital punishment, explained that probation

> is . . . a protection to the public and a restraint upon the probationer which in the case of a murderer can justifiably be retained indefinitely. While it is true that released murderers seldom offend again, there is often an element of instability in their character of temperament which tends to make them less reliable than others. There has been at least one case in the past where the conduct of a murderer on probation has caused such alarm in the neighbourhood that it became necessary to recall him until arrangements could be made for settling him elsewhere.[27]

But since the National Party had just been defeated in the general elections, Marshall concluded by noting that his successor might review his decision.

Marshall's successor was Mason, and he did indeed bring Mareo's case before Cabinet. Although Marshall had contended that a murderer should, except in 'exceptional cases', 'be on probation from the time of his release for the rest of his life',[28] Cabinet had requested information as to whether such a draconian policy had actually been implemented. The Secretary for Justice's figures would hearten today's advocates of law-and-order: four murderers had previously been discharged from probation but the most recent was as long ago as 1947.[29]

A week before Christmas 1958, Mareo was finally granted a discharge. He had been, to use his own phrase, 'under judicial control' for more than twenty-two years. Just under two years later his wife, Gladys Curtis, died. Within a few weeks Nora Bailey, the violinist and second 'Mrs Mareo', had flown to Auckland and married him. Nothing could have been more typical of the enigmatic life of the musician and composer. Mareo had left Nora Bailey and not seen her for twenty-eight years.

Was he heartlessly remarrying in order to exploit yet another woman a second time, or was he the kind of man who inspired extraordinary love and devotion? Perhaps time would have told, but for the fact that Mareo's fifth 'marriage' was to be his shortest. Less than a month after marrying Nora Bailey he died of heart failure.

Epilogue

A T THE TIME OF Mareo's death, Freda Stark was living in London, working at New Zealand House and moving in Chelsea gay and lesbian circles.[1] In 1970 she returned to New Zealand to enjoy, in addition to her previous incarnations as Star Witness and Fever of the Fleet, one final public role: New Zealand gay and lesbian 'icon'.

But for this to be possible the myth that she and Thelma were publicly recognised as 'lesbians' during the trials needed to be perpetuated. Obviously a lesbian who was 'out' in New Zealand during the 1930s would be a more interesting, or at least courageous, figure than one who wasn't. Accordingly, a TVNZ *One Tonight* show about Stark's attendance at a performance of a play in 1997 about her life claimed that '[a]fter public humiliation over her lesbian relationship, she vowed to never again take the stage',[2] and following her death in 1999, writer and film maker Peter Wells claimed in his obituary that 'Freda outed herself as a lesbian during the trial'.[3] A few years earlier, in an article about Wells's documentary *The Mighty Civic*, the *Women's Weekly* reported that

> [a]t a time when homosexuality was rarely discussed, and then only in whispers, Freda was upfront about her sexuality.
>
> 'I walked proud,' she says. 'Some people could be shocked at anything, but they respected my feelings.'
>
> After her photograph was published in the newspaper she was recognised whenever she went out. 'I would go into a shop and people would follow me in to see what I was buying. It wasn't so much because I was a lesbian, but that I was involved in a murder case. It was something for people to talk about.'[4]

More authoritatively, the entry on Stark in the *Dictionary of New Zealand Biography* states that '[d]uring the trial the relationship between Thelma and Freda became public'.[5]

Although Stark did make the significant admission to the *Women's Weekly* that people were less interested in her imputed lesbianism than her involvement in the trial, it is possible that she was unaware that she had distorted the truth both during and after the trials. Given the extraordinary pressures on her during them, she probably had to convince herself that she was telling the truth. Stark may not have spent the last sixty-three years of her life living with the awful knowledge that she had destroyed a friend's life and nearly sent him the gallows. Like Mareo, perhaps, she may have been something of a fantasist. Indeed, how could she not have been, given what she went through?

Similarly, while it defies common sense that Stark could have been both publicly recognised as a lesbian and trusted as a witness of unimpeachable virtue, it is nevertheless understandable that the gay and lesbian community should have turned her into an 'icon', to use Wells's description. The inaccuracies of Stark's testimony were in part due to the homophobia that has made it important to celebrate the lives of all gay men and lesbians who lived during those decades. Perhaps, then, it is ironically appropriate that some members of this community should be responsible in a very small way for continuing to perpetuate what we think is an injustice to Eric Mareo's memory. A persecuted social group is capable of small injustices, just as the society that nearly killed Mareo was also the one that produced the splendid but now largely forgotten cast of nonconformists, eccentrics and adversaries of prejudice that tenaciously defended him. In many ways the trials of Eric Mareo reflect the ways in which New Zealand was, and maybe still is, a society that epitomises both the strengths and weaknesses of middle-class, puritan values.

Notes

Abbreviations

EMP Eric Mareo Papers, Department of Justice, Wellington, New Zealand
MP   H.G.R. Mason Papers, MS-Papers-1751, Alexander Turnbull Library, Wellington, New Zealand
PF   Police Files on Eric Mareo, P1 1935/599, Archives New Zealand, Wellington
AS   *Auckland Star*
Dom *Dominion*
EP   *Evening Post*
NZH *New Zealand Herald*
Truth *New Zealand Truth*
Obs *Observer*
WN   *Weekly News*

Introduction

1 Notes of Evidence: *His Majesty the King* v. *Eric Mareo*, 17–26 February 1936 [First Trial Notes of Evidence], EMP, p.176.
2 *NZH*, 26 February 1936.
3 'Criticus' [Melville Harcourt], *I Appeal* (Auckland: Oswald-Sealy, 1945), p.71.
4 *AS*, 18 June 1936.
5 Mr Justice Callan to the Attorney-General, 24 June 1936, EMP.
6 See J.L. Robson, *Sacred Cows and Rogue Elephants: Policy Development in the New Zealand Justice Department* (Wellington: Government Printing Office, 1987), p.110.
7 Adele Bridgens, back cover of *Freda Stark: Her Extraordinary Life*, by Dianne Haworth and Diane Miller (Auckland: HarperCollins, 2000). Stark's biographers also tell the story of the Mareo trials but they rely almost entirely on contemporary newspaper reports and their subject's recollection of the events. Because they did not consult the Notes of Evidence of either of the trials, the various police reports and other archival material relevant to the case, there are some inaccuracies and numerous significant omissions in their account. The story needs to be retold if only to ensure accuracy and completion.
8 For a discussion of the many ways in which the law uses storytelling, see *Law's Stories: Narrative and Rhetoric in the Law*, edited by Peter Brooks and Paul Gewirtz, (New Haven: Yale University Press, 1996).

1 'A Very Experienced Man of the World': The Crown's Case

1 Mary Martin as quoted in John M. Thomson, *The Oxford History of New Zealand Music* (Auckland: Oxford University Press, 1991), p.145.

2 Maurice Hurst, *Music and the Stage in New Zealand: A Century of Entertainment,1840–1943* (Auckland: Charles Begg, 1944), p.9.

3 The classic account is Andreas Huyssen's *After the Great Divide: Modernism, Mass Culture, Postmodernism* (Bloomington: Indiana University Press, 1985). However, more recently the notion of an unbridgeable divide between high modernism and mass culture has been questioned by Michael Tratner, *Modernism and Mass Politics: Joyce, Woolf, Eliot, Yeats* (Stanford: Stanford University Press, 1995), the contributors to *High and Low Moderns: Literature and Culture, 1889–1939*, edited by Maria Di Battista and Lucy McDiarmid (New York: Oxford University Press, 1996) and Lawrence Rainey, *Institutions of Modernism: Literary Elites and Public Culture* (New Haven: Yale University Press, 1998).

4 Adrienne Simpson, *Opera's Farthest Frontier: A History of Professional Opera in New Zealand* (Auckland: Reed, 1996), p.164. For a discussion of the theatre and New Zealand musicals, see Peter Harcourt, *A Dramatic Appearance: New Zealand Theatre 1920–1970* (Wellington: Methuen, 1978), p.7–75 and *Fantasy and Folly: The Lost World of New Zealand Musicals, 1880–1940* (Wellington: Steele Roberts, 2002).

5 *Obs*, 7 & 14 September 1933.

6 *Obs*, 2 July 1936.

7 *Obs*, 22 September 1934.

8 *Obs*, 23 November 1933.

9 *Ibid.*

10 *New Zealand Radio Record*, 8 December 1933, p.15.

11 *Ibid.*

12 *Ibid.*

13 *NZH*, 22 September 1934.

14 *Obs*, 23 November 1933.

15 *Radio Record* 8 December1933, p.15.

16 *Obs*, 2 July 1936.

17 *Ibid.*

18 *Obs*, 13 September 1934.

19 Quoted by P. J. Gibbons, 'The Climate of Opinion', *Oxford History of New Zealand*, 2nd ed., edited by Geoffrey Rice (Auckland: Oxford University Press, 1992), p.321.

20 First Trial Notes of Evidence, EMP, pp.57–8.

21 First Trial Notes of Evidence, EMP, p.59.

22 *Ibid.*

23 First Trial Notes of Evidence, EMP, p.60.

24 *NZH*, 26 February 1936.

25 First Trial Notes of Evidence, EMP, p.26.

26 First Trial Notes of Evidence, EMP, p.60.

27 First Trial Notes of Evidence, EMP, p.28.
28 Statement to Police, 5 June 1936, EMP.
29 First Trial Notes of Evidence, EMP, p.60.
30 First Trial Notes of Evidence, EMP, p.19.
31 First Trial Notes of Evidence, EMP, pp.16, 18, 22.
32 First Trial Notes of Evidence, EMP, p.5.
33 PF, Part V.
34 *NZH*, 26 February 1936.
35 First Trial Notes of Evidence, EMP, p.62.
36 First Trial Notes of Evidence, EMP, pp.31, 32.
37 Statement to the Police, 15 April 1935, EMP.
38 *Ibid.*
39 First Trial Notes of Evidence, EMP, pp.36–7.
40 First Trial Notes of Evidence, EMP, p.63–4.
41 *Ibid.*
42 First Trial Notes of Evidence, EMP, p.64.
43 First Trial Notes of Evidence, EMP, p.65.
44 First Trial Notes of Evidence, EMP, pp.65–6.
45 First Trial Notes of Evidence, EMP, p.66.
46 First Trial Notes of Evidence, EMP, p.110.
47 First Trial Notes of Evidence, EMP, p.67.
48 *Ibid.*
49 First Trial Notes of Evidence, EMP, pp.69.
50 *Ibid.*
51 First Trial Notes of Evidence, EMP, p.70–1.
52 First Trial Notes of Evidence, EMP, p.187.
53 First Trial Notes of Evidence, EMP, p.174.
54 First Trial Notes of Evidence, EMP, p 175.
55 First Trial Notes of Evidence, EMP, pp.176.
56 First Trial Notes of Evidence, EMP, p.72.
57 First Trial Notes of Evidence, EMP, pp.109–10.
58 *NZH*, 26 February 1936.
59 First Trial Notes of Evidence, EMP, pp.177–8.
60 First Trial Notes of Evidence, EMP, pp.6–7.
61 First Trial Notes of Evidence, EMP, p.182.
62 First Trial Notes of Evidence, EMP, p.130.
63 *NZH*, 26 February 1936.

2 'Canned': Mareo's Defence

1 *NZH*, 26 February 1936.
2 First Trial Notes of Evidence, EMP, p.59.
3 Statement to the Police, 5 June 1936, EMP.
4 PF, Part V.
5 *Ibid.*
6 First Trial Notes of Evidence, EMP, p.58.

7 First Trial Notes of Evidence, EMP, p.11.
8 First Trial Notes of Evidence, EMP, p.8.
9 First Trial Notes of Evidence, EMP, p.61.
10 *NZH*, 26 February 1936.
11 MP, 3/12.
12 First Trial Notes of Evidence, EMP, pp.31, 32.
13 First Trial Notes of Evidence, EMP, p.31.
14 First Trial Notes of Evidence, EMP, p.101.
15 First Trial Notes of Evidence, EMP, p.104.
16 First Trial Notes of Evidence, EMP, p.119.
17 First Trial Notes of Evidence, EMP, p.126.
18 First Trial Notes of Evidence, EMP, p.103.
19 First Trial Notes of Evidence, EMP, p.175.
20 Statement to the Police, 19 April 1935, EMP.
21 *NZH*, 26 February 1936.
22 *Ibid.*
23 First Trial Notes of Evidence, EMP, p.176.
24 *Portrait of a Profession: The Centennial Book of the New Zealand Law Society*, edited by Robin Cooke (Wellington: Reed, 1969), p.175.
25 Sir Vincent Meredith, *A Long Brief: Recollections of a Crown Solicitor* (Auckland: Collins, 1966), p.123.
26 *NZH*, 27 February 1936.
27 First Trial Notes of Evidence, EMP, p.160.
28 First Trial Notes of Evidence, EMP, p.147.
29 First Trial Notes of Evidence, EMP, p.46.
30 First Trial Notes of Evidence, EMP, p.132.
31 First Trial Notes of Evidence, EMP, pp.169, 171.
32 First Trial Notes of Evidence, EMP, p.141.
33 First Trial Notes of Evidence, EMP, p.45.
34 First Trial Notes of Evidence, EMP, p.46.
35 First Trial Notes of Evidence, EMP, p.47.
36 First Trial Notes of Evidence, EMP, p.142.
37 First Trial Notes of Evidence, EMP, p.150.
38 First Trial Notes of Evidence, EMP, p.116.
39 First Trial Notes of Evidence, EMP, p.28.
40 First Trial Notes of Evidence, EMP, p.55.
41 First Trial Notes of Evidence, EMP, p.61.
42 *Ibid.*
43 First Trial Notes of Evidence, EMP, p.78.
44 Statement to the Police, 15 April 1935, EMP.
45 First Trial Notes of Evidence, EMP, p.175.
46 First Trial Notes of Evidence, EMP, p.8.
47 *NZH*, 27 February 1936.
48 *Ibid*; First Trial Notes of Evidence, EMP, p.183.
49 First Trial Notes of Evidence, EMP, p.129.
50 First Trial Notes of Evidence, EMP, p.167, 162.

51 Dr Chris Corns, *Anatomy of Long Criminal Trials* (Carlton South: Australian Institute of Judicial Administration Incorporated, 1997).

3   The Second Trial

1   Whitington to O'Leary, 18 February 1936, EMP.
2   Whitington to O'Leary, 19 February 1936, EMP.
3   O'Leary to the Minister of Justice, 5 March 1936, EMP.
4   *Ibid.*
5   Riano to O'Leary, 3 March 1936, EMP.
6   Statement to the Police by Dawson, 17 March 1936, EMP.
7   Statement to the Police by Hooper, 19 March 1936, EMP.
8   Statement to the Police by Kingsland, 17 March 1936, EMP.
9   Aekins to the Minister of Justice, 15 April 1936, EMP.
10 Notes of Evidence: *His Majesty the King* v. *Eric Mareo* 1–17 June, 1936. [Second Trial Notes of Evidence], EMP, pp.316.
11 *Portrait of a Profession*, p.223. On Meredith's hostility to Acheson, see R.P. Boast, 'Indigenous Peoples and the Law,' www.Kennett.co.nz/law/indigenous/1999/41.html.
12 Second Trial Notes of Evidence, EMP, p.229.
13 Second Trial Notes of Evidence, EMP, p.228.
14 Second Trial Notes of Evidence, EMP, pp.233, 237.
15 Second Trial Notes of Evidence, EMP, p.251.
16 Second Trial Notes of Evidence, EMP, p.239.
17 Second Trial Notes of Evidence, EMP, p.242.
18 Second Trial Notes of Evidence, EMP, p.258.
19 As even the Attorney-General, a layperson, was able discover during his research, MP.
20 Second Trial Notes of Evidence, EMP, p.171.
21 Second Trial Notes of Evidence, EMP, p.188.
22 Second Trial Notes of Evidence, EMP, p.198.
23 Second Trial Notes of Evidence, EMP, p.177.
24 Summing-up of Callan J., EMP, p.55.
25 Summing-up of Callan J., EMP, p.27.
26 Summing-up of Callan J., EMP, p.39.
27 Summing-up of Callan J., EMP, p.37.
28 Summing-up of Callan J., EMP, p.43.
29 Summing-up of Callan J., EMP, p.45.
30 Summing-up of Callan J., EMP, p.51.
31 Summing-up of Callan J., EMP, p.53.
32 Summing-up of Callan J., EMP, p.57.
33 *AS,* 18 June 1936.
34 *Ibid.*
35 *Ibid.*
36 *Portrait of a Profession*, p.130.
37 *AS,* 18 June 1936.

4 Who Was Eric Mareo?

1   *NZH* 15 February 1936.
2   *WN*, 12 February 1936.
3   *NZH*, 7 September 1935.
4   We are grateful to Allan Thomas for pointing out these names to us.
5   *Truth*, 15 July 1936.
6   *Obs*, 2 July 1936.
7   *Truth*, 8 July 1936.
8   PF, Part I.
9   *Obs*, 2 July 1936.
10 P.J. Gibbons, 'The Climate of Opinion,' *Oxford History of New Zealand*, p.336.
11 Tom Brooking, 'Economic Transformations,' *The Oxford History of New Zealand*, p.252.
12 Quoted in Tony Simpson, *The Sugarbag Years* (Auckland: Godwit, 1997), p.202.
13 Danielle Sprecher, 'Good Clothes are Good Business: Gender, Consumption and Appearance in the Office, 1918–39', *The Gendered Kiwi*, edited by Caroline Daley and Deborah Montgomerie (Auckland: Auckland University Press, 1999) p.149.
14 *Obs*, 13 September 1934.
15 R.A. Lochore, *From Europe to New Zealand: An Account of our Continental European Settlers* (Wellington: Reed, 1951), pp.13–14.
16 *Truth*, 4 March 1936.
17 *Ibid.*
18 Police Report on Eric Mareo, EMP.
19 PF, Part II.
20 K.C. Aekins to the Minister of Justice, 25 July 1936, EMP
21 Police Report on Eric Mareo, EMP.
22 PF, Part I.
23 PF, Part I.
24 Harcourt, *I Appeal*, pp.67–8.

5 The Lesbian Accusation

1   Statement to the Police, 5 June 1935, EMP.
2   PF, Part IV
3   Harcourt (*I Appeal*) does claim that during the first trial 'salaciously-minded females revelled in seeing rumours transformed into facts by the authoritative backing of the Crown. So the gossips were right after all. The information, which had been bandied round the town for months, threw a new light upon the relationships of the Mareos' (p.72). However, it was not 'stated' in court that she was a 'lesbian' and this was certainly not given 'the authoritative backing of the Crown'. It seems that in his enthusiasm for Mareo's cause, Harcourt wants to discredit not only these 'gossips' for spreading such a

rumour but also Thelma by verifying that it was true. In another book written after the trials the question of whether Thelma was a 'pervert' is raised but not answered. Richard Singer, *24 Notable Trials* (Auckland: Oswald-Sealy, 1944) p.126.

4   *Truth*, 4 March 1936.

5   *NZH*, 26 February 1936.

6   *AS*, 16 June 1936.

7   *NZH*, 27 February 1936.

8   Edward Shorter, *From the Mind into the Body: The Cultural Origins of Psychosomatic Symptoms* (Toronto: Maxwell Macmillan, 1994), pp.42, 44.

9   First Trial Notes of Evidence, EMP, p.51.

10 First Trial Notes of Evidence, EMP, p.28.

11 First Trial Notes of Evidence, EMP, pp.80–1.

12 First Trial Notes of Evidence, EMP, p.9.

13 First Trial Notes of Evidence, EMP, p.80.

14 First Trial Notes of Evidence, EMP, p.52.

15 First Trial Notes of Evidence, EMP, p.83.

16 PF, Part V

17 First Trial Notes of Evidence, EMP, p.29.

18 Second Trial Notes of Evidence, EMP, p.215.

19 Second Trial Notes of Evidence, EMP, p.91.

20 Julie Glamuzina and Alison Laurie, *Parker & Hulme: A Lesbian View* (Ithaca, NY: Firebrand Books, 1995), p.160.

21 Glamuzina and Laurie, *Parker & Hulme*, pp.158, 150.

22 Riano to O'Leary, 3 March 1936, EMP.

23 Jeffrey Weeks, *Coming Out: Homosexual Politics in Britain from the Nineteenth Century to the Present* (London, New York: Quartet Books, 1977), p.12. See also Michel Foucault, *The History of Sexuality: Volume 1: An Introduction*, trans. Robert Hurley, (New York: Vintage, 1980), pp.43, 101.

24 George Chauncey, 'Christian Brotherhood or Sexual Perversion? Homosexual Identities and the Construction of Sexual Boundaries in the World War One Era', *Hidden from History: Reclaiming the Gay and Lesbian Past*, edited by Martin Bauml Duberman, Martha Vicinus, and George Chauncey (New York: New American Library, 1989), pp.294–317.

25 Weeks, *Coming Out*, p.12.

26 Stevan Eldred-Grigg, *Pleasures of the Flesh: Sex & Drugs in Colonial New Zealand* (Wellington: Reed, 1984), p.124.

27 Report by Sir William Willcox, EMP.

28 P.P. Lynch to the Under-Secretary for the Department of Justice, 2 December 1941, EMP.

29 Quoted by Neil Miller, *Out of the Past: Gay and Lesbian History from 1869 to the Present* (New York: Vintage, 1995), p.26.

30 *Mental Health and the Community*, edited by P.J. Lawrence (Christchurch: Canterbury Mental Health Council, 1963), p.373.

31 Second Trial Notes of Evidence, EMP, p.251.

32 Quoted by Miller, *Out of the Past*, p.190. For a recent account of the trials, see Diana Southami, *The Trials of Radclyffe Hall* (London: Virago, 1999).
33 Second Trial Notes of Evidence, EMP, p.254.
34 *Truth*, 18 March 1936.
35 See Julie Glamuzina, 'An Outstanding Masquerade', and Jenny Coleman, 'Unsettled Women: Deviant Genders in Late Nineteenth and Early Twentieth-Century New Zealand', *Lesbian Studies in Aotearoa/New Zealand*, edited by Alison J. Laurie (Binghamton, NY: Harrington, 2001).
36 Lillian Faderman, *Odd Girls and Twilight Lovers: A History of Lesbian Life in Twentieth-Century America* (London: Penguin, 1992), p.48.
37 Faderman, *Odd Girls*, p.1.
38 Faderman, *Odd Girls*, pp.13, 14.
39 See Sally Irwin, *Between Heaven and Earth: The Life of a Mountaineer, Freda Du Faur 1882–1935* (Melbourne: White Crane Press, 2000), p.283–5. See also Aorewa McLeod, 'New Zealand's Lost Lesbian Writers and Artists', Alison J. Laurie, 'Frances Mary Hodgkins: Journeys into the Hearts of Women', and Jenny Coleman 'Unsettled Women: Deviant Genders in Late Nineteenth and Early Twentieth-Century New Zealand', *Lesbian Studies in Aotearoa/New Zealand*.
40 *Truth*, 18 March 1936.
41 *Boston Marriages: Romantic but Asexual Relationships among Contemporary Lesbians*, edited by Esther D. Rothblum and Kathleen A. Brehony (Amherst: University of Massachusetts Press, 1993), p.34–5.
42 PF, Part V.

6 A Pharmakon, a Pharmakos and a Pure Woman

1 Second Trial Notes of Evidence, EMP, p.134.
2 Second Trial Notes of Evidence, EMP, p.146.
3 For some influential near-contemporary accounts of New Zealand puritanism, see E.H. McCormick, *Letters and Art in New Zealand* (Wellington: Department of Internal Affairs, 1940), Bill Pearson, 'Fretful Sleepers', *Landfall*, 6 (1952): 201–30 and R.M. Chapman, 'Fiction and the Social Pattern', *Landfall*, 7 (1953): 26–58. For a discussion of Puritanism and counter-puritanism before the First World War, see Eldred-Grigg, *Pleasures of the Flesh*. Although Eldred-Grigg attempts to counter the perception of New Zealand as an unusually puritan country it is significant that his history does not extend past 1915 when, arguably, 'puritanism' was at its height.
4 Phillida Bunkle, 'The Origins of the Women's Movement in New Zealand: The Women's Christian Temperance Union 1885–1895', *Women in New Zealand Society*, edited by Phillida Bunkle and Beryl Hughes (Boston: Allen and Unwin, 1980), p.72. See also Raewyn Dalziel 'The Colonial Helpmeet: Women's Role and the Vote in Nineteenth Century New Zealand', *Women in History: Essays on European Women in New Zealand*, edited by Barbara Brookes, Charlotte Macdonald and Margaret Tennant (Wellington: Allen and Unwin/Port Nicholson Press, 1986), pp.55–68 and Barbara Brookes, 'A

Weakness for Strong Subjects', *New Zealand Journal of History* 27 (1993): 140–56.

5   Erik Olssen, 'Families and the Gendering of European New Zealand in the Colonial Period, 1840–80', *The Gendered Kiwi*, p.54. For an earlier discussion of the post-colonial period, see the same author's 'Women, Work and Family: 1880–1926' in *Women in New Zealand Society* pp.159–83.

6   This at least was the case in Australia, according to Ann Summers in her classic *Damned Whores and God's Police* (Ringwood, Vic: Penguin, 1994).

7   Roberta Nicholls, *The Women's Parliament: The National Council of Women of New Zealand 1896–1920* (Wellington: Victoria University Press, 1996), pp.68–88 and Dorothy Page, *The National Council of Women: A Centennial History* (Auckland: Auckland University Press, 1996). However Charlotte Macdonald has countered what she calls the '"the black hole" of New Zealand's feminist history' between the first and the second 'waves' of feminism, in *The Vote, the Pill and the Demon Drink: A History of Feminist Writing in New Zealand, 1869–1993* (Wellington: Bridget Williams Books, 1993), p.8. On the conservative aspects of the Plunket Society, see Erik Olssen, 'Truby King and the Plunket Society: An Analysis of a Prescriptive Ideology,' *New Zealand Journal of History* 15 (1981): 3–23.

8   Quoted in Sue Kedgley, *Mum's the Word* (Auckland: Random House, 1996), p.115. Of course it has been argued that the gender imbalance of nineteenth-century New Zealand society resulted in a masculinist society. However, there is no logical reason why a gender imbalance could not create the cultural conditions where both highly 'feminine' and 'masculine' values could thrive. A relative absence of women would make 'feminine' virtues desirable by virtue of their scarcity and unmarried men and their 'batchelor' values commonplace by virtue of their numerical predominance. For the case that the gender imbalance created a 'man's country', see Jock Phillips, *A Man's Country? The Image of the Pakeha Male*, revised ed. (Auckland: Auckland University Press, 1996), pp.4–11. For the contrary position, see Raewyn Dalziel, 'The Colonial Helpmeet: Women's Role and the Vote in Nineteenth-Century New Zealand', in *Women in History*, pp.55–68 and for the skeptical position about the effects of the gender imbalance see Charlotte Macdonald, 'Too Many Men and Too Few Women: Gender's "Fatal Impact" in Nineteenth-Century Colonies', in *The Gendered Kiwi*, p.28.

9   *AS*, 17 June 1936.

10 Meredith, *A Long Brief*, p.96.

11 John Parascandola, *Drugs and Narcotics in History*, edited by Roy Porter and Mikulas Teich (Cambridge: Cambridge University Press, 1995), p.156.

12 See Derek Challis and Gloria Rawlinson, *The Book of Iris: A Life of Robin Hyde* (Auckland: Auckland University Press, 2002), p.189. We are grateful to Fergus Barrowman for pointing this out. Hyde's article is reprinted in *Disputed Ground: Robin Hyde, Journalist*, introduced and selected by Gillian Boddy & Jacqueline Matthews (Wellington: Victoria University Press, 1991), p.257.

13 Charles Raymond Henwood, *A Turned on World: Drug use in New Zealand*

(Wellington: Hicks Smith, 1971), p.61. See also Redmer Yska, *New Zealand Green: The Story of Marijuana in New Zealand* (Auckland: Bateman, 1990), pp.7–34.

14 Parascandola, *Drugs and Narcotics in History*, p.160.

15 Harcourt, *I Appeal*, p.72. For the association of drugs and bohemianism during the postwar period, see Marek Kohn, *Dope Girls: The Birth of the British Drug Underground* (London: Lawrence & Wishart, 1992).

16 See Zygmunt Baumann's description of 'proteophobia' as 'the apprehension and vexation related not to something or someone disquieting through otherness and unfamiliarity, but to something or someone that does not fit the structure of the orderly world, does not fall easily into any of the established categories' and his argument that '"the Jews"' in antisemitic discourse 'incarnate' the kind of 'ambivalence' that occasions such 'proteophobia' in 'Allosemitism: Premodern, Modern, Postmodern' in *Modernity, Culture and 'the Jew'*, edited by Bryan Cheyette and Laura Marcus (Cambridge: Polity Press, 1998), p.144.

17 Harcourt, *I Appeal*, p.68.

18 Helen Blagrove to the Minister of Justice, 1 July 1936, EMP.

19 *NZH*, 26 February 1936.

20 *Truth*, 18 March 1936.

21 First Trial Notes of Evidence, EMP, p.29.

22 Harcourt, *I Appeal*, p.67.

23 'I Appeal' by 'Criticus': A Review, EMP.

24 *Obs*, 9 July 1936.

25 Quoted in Barbara Brookes, 'Housewives' Depression: The Debate over Abortion and Birth Control in the 1930s', *New Zealand Journal of History* 15 (1981), p.130.

26 Brookes, 'Housewives' Depression', 122n. See also Phillipa Mein Smith, *Maternity in Dispute: New Zealand, 1920–1939* (Wellington: Historical Publications Branch, 1986), pp.101–15 and Mary Dobbie, *A Matter for Women: Early Years of the Family Planning Movement* (Auckland: Family Planning Association, 1995).

27 *Truth*, 24 June 1936.

28 *Ibid.*

29 Aekins to the Governor-General, 14 July 1936, EMP.

30 *Truth*, 24 June 1936.

31 See Bronwyn Dalley, 'Criminal Conversations: Infanticide, Gender and Sexuality in Nineteenth-Century New Zealand', *The Gendered Kiwi*, pp.63–86 and 'The Cultural Remains of Elsie Walker', *Fragments: New Zealand Social and Cultural History*, edited by Bronwyn Dalley and Bronwyn Labrun (Auckland: Auckland University Press, 2000), pp.140–62.

32 See Kai Jensen, *Whole Men: The Masculine Tradition in New Zealand Literature* (Auckland: Auckland University Press, 1996) for a discussion of this literary tradition and more generally *Gender, Culture and Power: Challenging New Zealand's Gendered Culture*, edited by Bev James and Kay Saville-Smith (Auckland: Oxford University Press, 1989) Phillips, *A Man's*

Country? and *Masculinities in Aotearoa/New Zealand,* edited by Robin Law, Hugh Campbell and John Dolan (Palmerston North: Dunmore Press, 1999).

7 In the Condemned Cell

1 Geoffrey Robertson, *The Justice Game* (London: Chatto & Windus, 1998), p.97.

2 This was at least the official rationale for the speedy dispatch of convicted murderers. Robertson QC gives the real reason as being '. . . to emphasise the deterrent effect of punishment which followed so soon after the exposure of the facts of the crime in court' and also '. . . to ensure that no campaign of sympathy for the criminal had time to build up a head of steam.' *The Justice Game,* p.75.

3 These are actually the written words of Melville Harcourt who wrote an unconventional biography of Moreton that takes the conceit of being an autobiography, *A Parson in Prison: A Biography of the Rev. George Edgar Moreton* (Auckland: Whitcombe & Tombs, 1942), pp.182, 298.

4 Mareo to O'Leary, 2 July 1936.

5 *Truth,* 1 July 1936.

6 *Ibid.*

7 A Mother to Mason, 8 July 1936, EMP.

8 Harcourt, *I Appeal,* pp.70, 72.

9 Petition to the Minister of Justice, 16 July 1936, EMP.

10 Press interest was sparked it seems by a leader in the *Christchurch Star Sun* on 28 February 1936. See for example the subsequent editorials in the *Greymouth Evening Star,* 29 February 1936 and the *Wanganui Chronical,* 4 March 1936 and Pauline Engel, *The Abolition of Capital Punishment in New Zealand,* 1935–1961 (Wellington: Dept. of Justice, 1977), pp.10–17, from whom these references have been taken.

11 *WN,* 4 March 1936.

12 Quoted in Engel, *The Abolition of Capital Punishment,* p.12.

13 *Ibid.*

14 *Truth,* 24 June 1936.

15 Sherwood Young, *Guilty on the Gallows: Famous Capital Crimes of New Zealand* (Wellington: Grantham House, 1998), p.9.

16 Callan to the Attorney-General, 24 June 1936, EMP.

17 *Ibid.*

18 O'Leary to Mason, 24 July 1936, EMP.

19 Meredith to the Solicitor-General, 26 July 1936, EMP.

20 Elizabeth Mareo to Mason, 26 June 1936, EMP.

21 Quoted in Greg Newbold, *Punishment and Politics: The Maximum Security Prison in New Zealand* (Auckland: Oxford University Press, 1989), p.7.

22 Dallard to Mason, 17 July 1936, EMP.

23 *Ibid.*

24 Who were: the Right Hon. M.J. Savage, Hon. P. Fraser, Hon. W. Nash, Hon. D.G. Sullivan, Hon. H.T. Armstrong, Hon. R. Semple, Hon. W.E. Parry, Hon.

P.C. Webb, Hon. F. Jones, Hon. W. Lee Martin, Hon. F. Langstone and Hon. M. Fagan.

25 *Truth,* 12 August 1936. By way of addendum, the death penalty for murder was not abolished until 1941 when, somewhat bizarrely, amending legislation was rushed through the house in order to avoid a potential constitutional crisis. The then Governor-General, Sir Cyril Newall, indicated that he would refuse to act on the advice of Cabinet that a sentence of flogging which had been imposed on four prisoners at Mt Eden should be remitted. He did so not because he was an advocate of corporal punishment (he was not) but because he considered it to be constitutionally improper for the Executive to override the will of Parliament (as expressed in the form of statutory penalties for certain offences) in this way. Of course the same constitutional objection could be made to the Executive's long-standing practice in relation to capital cases. In any event, the Government's solution was to announce that it was shortly to introduce a bill abolishing flogging. And as the issues of corporal and capital punishment had always been regarded by the Labour Party as inextricably linked, it followed that the amendment would, and did, also proscribe the death penalty. Equally strangely – in light of Mason's oft repeated comments that abolition was one matter upon which the Labour Party would not tolerate dissent – the amending legislation was deliberately introduced and passed while the Prime Minister, Peter Fraser, was overseas, apparently in the knowledge that it might well not have been supported by him. In the following years, which saw the reintroduction of the death penalty by a National Government and its abolition again as a result of the passage of the Crimes Bill 1961, the Mareo case was often cited by proponents of abolition in support of their arguments.

8 'J'Accuse': Facts and Phalluses

1 Holmes to the Minister of Justice, 28 August 1942, EMP.
2 Department of Health to Dallard, 21 July 1936, EMP.
3 PF, Part IV.
4 Sir Douglas Robb, Foreword, *Doctor Smith: Hokianga's 'King of the North'*, by G. Kemble Welch (Auckland: Blackwood & Janet Paul, 1965), p.17.
5 G.M. Smith, *Notes from a Backblock Hospital* (Christchurch: The Caxton Press, 1938).
6 PF, Part IV.
7 Dallard to Mason, 8 July 1942, EMP. In his book of personal reminiscences published in 1938, *Notes from a Backblock Hospital*, Smith provided an extended analysis of the trials and the inadequacy of the Crown's medical witnesses.
8 Opinion of Mr Edward G. Hemmerde, 4 October 1940, MP, 3/11.
9 Willcox Report, 4 July 1941, EMP.
10 PF, Part V.
11 Petition to the Prisons Board, 29 April 1943, EMP.
12 Barry Gustafson, *Dictionary of New Zealand Biography*, Vol. 4, 1921–1940,

edited by Claudia Orange (Auckland: Auckland University Press, 1998), p.444–5.

13 Statutory Declaration by Dr Roche Lynch, EMP.

14 PF, Part II.

15 Notes Re Mareo by H.G.R. Mason, undated, EMP.

16 PF, Part III.

17 Second Trial Notes of Evidence, EMP, p.57.

18 PF, Part I.

19 *Ibid.*

20 Second Trial Notes of Evidence, EMP, p.120.

21 PF, Part III.

22 Memorandum to Cabinet, March 1945, MP, 3/8.

23 Harcourt, *I Appeal*, pp.56, 58.

24 Nancy M. Taylor, *The Home Front*, Vol. 1 of the *Official History of New Zealand in the Second World War 1939–45* (Wellington: Government Printer, 1986), p.246.

25 PF, Part I.

26 *Ibid.*

27 *Ibid.*

9 A 'Topper' in Mt Eden Gaol

1 *Truth*, 9 June 1937.

2 *Truth*, 31 January 1940.

3 The Superintendent of Mt Eden Goal to the Controller-General of Prisons, 31 October 1936, EMP.

4 Pechotsch to Dallard, 30 November 1936, EMP.

5 Pechotsch to Dallard, 30 December 1936, EMP.

6 Harcourt, *A Parson in Prison*, p.299.

7 Singer, *24 Notable Trials*, pp.122, 123.

8 Doidge to Mason, 14 February 1943, EMP.

9 *New Zealand Parliamentary Debates*, Vol. 261, 4 December 1942, pp.944–6.

10 *Parliamentary Debates*, Vol. 261, p.945.

11 Second Trial Notes of Evidence, EMP, p.214.

12 *Parliamentary Debates*, Vol. 261, p.945.

13 *Parliamentary Debates*, Vol. 261, pp.944–5.

14 *Parliamentary Debates*, Vol. 261, p.946.

15 Sexton to Harker, 13 August 1943, MP, 3/8.

16 *New Zealand Parliamentary Debates*, Vol. 263, 25 August 1943, p.1019.

17 *Parliamentary Debates,* Vol. 263, pp.1019–20.

18 Dallard to Mason, 8 July 1942, EMP.

19 As quoted by Dallard to the Clerk of the Statutes Revision Committee, 21 September 1942.

20 Statement by Philip Patrick Lynch, 16 October 1944, EMP.

21 PF, Part II.

22 *Ibid.*

23 Statement by Philip Patrick Lynch, 16 October 1944, EMP. Dr Lynch would later republish a barely edited version of his report in *No Remedy for Death: The Memoirs of a Pathologist* (London: John Long, 1970), pp.115–26. In a private letter to Mrs Eleanor Spragg (née Brownlee) Mason claimed that 'Dr. Lynch's book gives a story quite contrary to fact and to uncontradicted trial evidence,' 1 October 1971, MP, 3/8.

24 PF, Part III.

25 Dallard to Meredith, 6 November 1942, EMP.

26 Mason to Dallard, 22 December 1942, EMP.

27 Mason to Dallard, 18 January 1943, EMP.

28 Mason to Dallard, 22 December 1942, EMP.

29 *New Zealand Parliamentary Debates*, Vol. 263, p.1018.

30 Mason to the Solicitor-General, 7 June 1945, MP, 3/12.

31 Dallard to 'Phil', 24 February 1943, EMP.

32 Mason to Dallard, 24 February 1943, EMP.

33 Dallard to Mason, 5 March 1943, EMP. The following year Dallard had fallen out with his minister again on a matter unrelated to the Mareo case. Following a long exchange of letters in the *Hawera Star*, Mason wrote in a minute: 'By turning the matter into a personal combat you desert an unassailable position for an impossible one. Please send no further communications to the press in reference to prison matters without reference to me.' Quoted in J.L. Robson, *Sacred Cows and Rogue Elephants*, p.46.

34 Minutes of the Prisons Board, 28 November 1944, EMP.

35 Harcourt, *A Parson in Prison*, p.302.

36 Minutes of the Prisons Board, 28 November 1944, EMP.

37 Petition for Release of Eric Mareo, 11 April 1945, EMP.

38 Eve to Mareo, 21 April 1945, EMP.

39 Superintendent of Mt Eden Goal to Dallard, 7 May 1945, EMP.

40 Dallard to Schramm, 23 July 1945, EMP.

41 H.E. Evans to Mason, 25 June 1945, MP, 3/12.

42 'I Appeal' by 'Criticus': A Review, EMP.

43 *The King* v. *Mareo (No. 3)*, 10–13, 15, 16 April; 19 June 1946. Court of Appeal, Wellington. NZLR 669.

44 *The King* v. *Mareo (No. 3)*, pp.671, 673, 674.

45 *The King* v. *Mareo (No. 3)*, pp.671–2.

46 AS, 17 June 1936.

47 EP, 10 April 1946.

48 *The King* v. *Mareo (No. 3)*, p.673.

10 Golden Years

1 Trott to Dallard, 26 December 1946, EMP.

2 Dallard to Trott, 11 December 1946, EMP.

3 Trott to Dallard, 6 February 1947, EMP.

4 *Truth*, 1 October 1947.

5 *New Zealand Parliamentary Debates,* Vol. 278, 7 October 1947, pp.693–4.
6 *Truth,* 15 October 1947.
7 *Truth,* 19 May 1948.
8 *Ibid.*
9 *Truth,* 23 June 1948.
10 Dallard to the Chief Probation Officer, 28 July 1948, EMP.
11 The Chief Probation Officer to Dallard, 30 July 1948, EMP.
12 Doctor's Report on Mareo's Health, 24 May 1949, EMP.
13 Mareo to Dallard, 27 May 1949, EMP.
14 Dallard to Mareo, 31 May 1949, EMP.
15 Mareo to the Minister of Justice, 17 October 1950, EMP.
16 Probation Report, 16 October 1950, EMP.
17 The Probation Officer to the Secretary for Justice, 23 May 1951, EMP.
18 The Probation Officer to the Secretary for Justice, 18 May 1955, EMP.
19 *NZH,* 9 August 1951; *AS,* 9 August 1951.
20 *NZ Listener,* 15 September 1953.
21 *Ibid.*
22 *NZ Listener,* 23 October 1953.
23 *Press,* 23 October 1953.
24 According to a letter from Mareo's probation officer to the Secretary for Justice, 7 June 1957, EMP.
25 Mareo to the Chairman and Members of the Prisons Board, 1 May 1955, EMP.
26 Probationer Officer to the Secretary for Justice, 7 June 1957, EMP.
27 Marshall to the Chief Justice, 4 December 1957, EMP.
28 *Ibid.*
29 The Secretary for Justice to Mason, 9 December 1958, EMP.

Epilogue

1 Haworth and Miller, *Freda Stark,* pp.128–31.
2 TVNZ *One Tonight,* 17 February 1997. However, the *Listener* reported that 'Stark gave evidence in court against him, carefully skirting around her relationship with the singer. [Amanda Rees, the author of the play] said that "[i]n those days, if she was seen as gay, she would have been characterised as an unreliable witness and unable to testify. And she was the only witness."' Louise Reynolds, 'Gilt Complex', *Listener,* 15 February 1997. We did not attend any of the performances of Amanda Rees's play and the author would not grant us permission to read any of her scripts.
3 Peter Wells, 'Freda Stark: 23 March 1910–19 March 1999', *Express: New Zealand's Newspaper of Gay Expression,* 1 April 1999.
4 Donna Fleming, 'Murder, forbidden love – what a past!', *New Zealand Women's Weekly,* 17 January 1994.
5 Shirley Hodsell Williams, *Dictionary of New Zealand Biography,* Vol. 5, p.494.

Index